investing in stocks

10 MINUTE GUIDE

alpha books
201 West 103rd Street
Indianapolis, IN 46290

A Pearson Education Company

E. Alexander Saenz

10 Minute Guide to Investing in Stocks

Copyright © 2000 by Alpha Books

International Standard Book Number: 0-02-863610-4
Library of Congress Catalog Card Number: Available upon request.

03   02   01   8   7   6   5   4   3

Interpretation of the printing code: The rightmost number of the first series of numbers is the year of the book's printing; the rightmost number of the second series of numbers is the number of the book's printing. For example, a printing code of 00-1 shows that the first printing occurred in 2000.

Printed in the United States of America

Trademarks

This book is dedicated to Martin Saenz, who gave me my first dollar, and to Ed Saenz, who taught me the rest of them wouldn't come so easily.

Contents

Introduction

The current explosion of the stock market is unprecedented by any period in its history. Since the 1980s, the number of American households that own common stock has risen from below 20 percent to just under half. And, this does not include households that hold stock within their retirement plans or other indirect means. A significant portion of this growth is a direct result of the proliferation of information available to the public through such new forums as the Internet. Any information without explanation, however, is useless.

As a result, many people view the stock market as the domain of number crunchers who speak in a foreign language and do things the average person couldn't begin to understand. This lack of understanding often leads the person on the street into the arms of a financial professional to manage his or her money. This in itself is not necessarily bad. Many people, however, are surprised to discover that with a minimum of effort, they can become fully qualified to handle their investments themselves, much as they handle their other finances. In addition, people who have hired someone to manage financial matters for them place themselves in a particularly vulnerable position if they do not have even the most rudimentary understanding of how their money is being managed.

That's where this book comes in. The major aim of this book is to explain the basics of stock market investing in language that is understandable to the reader. To that extent, this book is full of comparisons to other everyday situations, anecdotes, personal experiences, and even strange-but-true facts to keep you interested as you make your way through the wonderful world of personal investing.

Like a map, this book will guide you through the investing maze while giving you a heads-up for the things you should pay particular attention to, ignore, or use to determine your own level of interest. This book is not intended to be a textbook nor a comprehensive reference, but rather to give you more than sufficient information to get started as an investor. That in itself has proven time and time again to be enough to whet the average investor's appetite to know more. Good luck to you, and happy investing.

EXTRAS

There are many things to learn before investing in the stock market. Use the vital information in the chapters to guide you in your investment decisions. Scattered throughout the pages are sidebars with useful information, definitions of financial terms, helpful tips, and cautions to help you handle your investments.

PLAIN ENGLISH

> This sidebar defines investing terms and basic concepts.

TIP

> Here you'll find tips on how to make investment decisions.

CAUTION

> Take these sidebars seriously—they help you avoid investing mistakes.

ACKNOWLEDGMENTS

There is no shortage of people who have helped me immensely in the writing of this book. I am indebted and very grateful to them all. If I've forgotten anyone, please know that it is unintentional. Thank you to Renee Wilmeth for having the patience of a saint and to Joan Paterson who is hands down the best editor I've ever had the privilege of working with. A very special thanks to Tony Vlamis, Florence Stone, and Tom O'Neil who believed in a young business writer and gave me more opportunities and help than I can ever repay. Thanks to mom and dad for their constant belief in and support of me. Thanks also to my brother, Art, and sister, Tina, for having enough humor to let me use them as examples. Thanks also to Tias Be-Be and Henri for betting on the dark horse.

LESSON 1

Confronting Your
Fear of Stocks

In this lesson you will learn what stock market investing really entails as opposed to common myths you may have heard.

WHAT YOU NEED TO KNOW BEFORE BEGINNING

Welcome to the world of investing in the stock market. You are about to join the ranks of a very elite group of people, namely those who have decided to actively manage their own money and make it work for them. This is a big step, and not one that should be taken without sufficient preparation. Before beginning with the more technical aspects of investing in the stock market, then, you should first ensure you have dealt with any mitigating circumstances that might otherwise distract you.

TIP

Many outside factors, such as lack of cash and preexisting fears, may affect your investment abilities and decisions. Learn about your fears before attempting to invest.

The most obvious confounding circumstance would be lack of cash with which to invest. The effects of this situation would probably be limited, however, to a lack of opportunity for profit. Also significant would be a lack of understanding of how stocks compare with other investments. That is explained here sufficiently to neutralize that fear.

More insidious, however, are the preexisting fears many people bring with them. These fears can affect investment decisions up to and including the decision whether to invest at all. Here are some common ones:

- Fear of technical-ese

- Fear that your financial knowledge is insufficient

- Fear that investing is only for millionaires

- Fear of stock market crashes

- Fear that investing in the stock market is a gamble

- Fear that investing is too time-consuming

Because these fears have the potential for damage, it's best to meet them head on. Face your fears of the stock market directly by learning the truths behind erroneous information you may have heard. You will then be able to place any reservations you may have had in their proper perspectives.

TECHNICAL-ESE

The stock market has a language all its own—street talk. Terms like zero-coupon bonds, net asset values, and price/earnings ratios are absolutely guaranteed to draw a blank look from the average person on the street. This shouldn't be surprising. Every trade, sport, and craft has a certain number of terms or phrases that are unique to it. And, since language is created by need, specific terms have arisen in each sphere to address this need for description.

TIP

> To deal with the fear of technical-ese, or the terminology used in the financial community, keep in mind that as a beginning investor your need for learning these terms is limited.

The terminology used in some areas, in sports for example, is familiar to almost everyone. Most people know what a seventh-inning stretch, a free throw, and a touchdown are even if they've never played or attended a game in their lives. However, in other areas, such as law and medicine, the terminology seems confusing and technical, leading to the general consensus that much schooling and substantial intellectual ability are required to understand any of it.

Unfortunately, finance—which includes the stock market—has long fallen into that second category. There could be several reasons why. Perhaps one is the fact that much of finance involves math—and we all know how we struggled with that in high school. Perhaps it is because Wall Street's conservative image makes us uncomfortable and thus we don't pretend to understand what it's about and we are hesitant to ask.

TIP

> While the sheer number of financial terms might be a little overwhelming, learning them isn't as daunting a task as it might appear. Many basic terms are used very frequently and will quickly become familiar.

For the longest time, and to some extent even today, the financial community was dependent on mass ignorance to survive. For example, let's take the term "investment management." This term means just that, the management of investments. Under normal circumstances, the average person certainly wouldn't trust someone else to take care of everything he or she owned. So, investment managers, brokers, and financial analysts regularly tossed out terms that they knew their clients wouldn't understand. Since no one wanted to appear stupid, the clients would simply nod their heads a lot and be grateful that someone was around who could interpret all these obscure terms. By intimidating their clients this way, investment managers kept their clients from realizing investment management was little more complicated than the management of their household finances, which the clients were already doing themselves. Should the masses ever wise up and begin to manage their investments themselves, the jobs of the investment managers would disappear.

In all fairness, however, there are a significant number of specialized terms used in the stock market—the world of finance has to be described somehow. The financial community is directly involved in almost every aspect of every person's life on the globe today; it employs hundreds of millions of people and is comprised of every industry in existence. Trying to describe all that this includes is going to take a lot of words. But, happily, you certainly don't need to know all the terms in order to be a successful investor. I am a longtime professional financial writer, and I still look things up. All you need to learn are the terms that are relevant to you. And this book is a good place to start. In addition, by gaining a working knowledge of investment terminology, you will be able to manage your own investments should you choose to, just as you manage your own household finances and paycheck. After all, who is better equipped to make decisions regarding your money than you?

As the terms rise in complexity, they are less familiar even to seasoned financial veterans. For example, the percentage of customers in a bar who order a basic drink like a martini will be pretty high. In much the same way, certain words will prove to be the basis for describing your particular financial investments. When a customer orders something strange like a Screaming Viking, the bartender will need to look up that drink recipe or simply ask the customer what is in it. Similarly, when hit with a term you don't understand, you can either look it up or ask someone to explain it to you. By the way, don't be embarrassed to do this. I haven't met anyone yet who doesn't love the opportunity to expound on what he or she knows about stocks. Also, you'll never need to ask again.

INSUFFICIENT FINANCIAL KNOWLEDGE

Not understanding the workings of financial markets, such as the stock market, is comparable to not understanding financial terms, but the potential for getting into trouble is much greater. A lack of knowledge when you invest in the stock market can get you financially wiped out. Here are two tips for obtaining the knowledge needed to be a successful investor:

1. Up to now you have probably had little or no reason to learn about the workings of the stock market. Until the time I decided to take sky diving lessons, I couldn't have told you at what altitude the cord must be pulled. Before I took my first plunge, however, I assure you I was *very* sure of when I was supposed to pull my chute. In much the same fashion, you should learn everything you can before taking the investment plunge.

2. As with the technical terms, you only have to learn the workings of those investments that pertain to you.

TIP

If you feel intimidated by financial information, the best way to deal with it is to casually scan through the financial media. Pick up a copy of *The Wall Street Journal* or watch *Moneyline* on TV. You'll be surprised to discover that you understand a lot more than you thought you would.

This book is designed to explain the internal processes of the stock market that are relevant to you the investor. It will not overwhelm you with extraneous information but instead will give you the essential information you need to know to get started as an investor. Over the years I have learned such informational tidbits regarding the workings of the stock market as how stocks are coded into various classes, how trades are settled, and how to recognize the various functions of the floor traders from the colors of their coats. All of this is certainly interesting and often fun information; however, the color of a floor trader's coat will in no way help you make intelligent investment decisions.

There's an old phrase that sums up expertise quite nicely, "Everything is easy ... if you know how." With that in mind, this book attempts to explain some of the more esoteric functions in terms and with examples that are familiar to the average person. The real responsibility of understanding these functions, however, is up to you, the individual investor. This is important because, as like any industry, the stock market has unscrupulous people who prey on uninformed investors. The golden rule of investing, therefore, is "Know what you are getting yourself into." Only by arming yourself with knowledge can you ensure that you will not be taken advantage of or make a bad decision.

IT'S NOT THAT DIFFICULT

Fortunately, expanding your financial knowledge is not hard. Repeated exposure will make many of these things increasingly familiar. So, here are some good ways to increase your knowledge:

- Listen to the financial news.

- Look at the stock pages.

- Check out financial Web sites.

Do these activities even when you do not understand what is being discussed. Initially, this may prove a little frustrating, but over time you will begin to develop an understanding that will become your knowledge base. Soon you will be able to ask the appropriate questions needed to gain a fuller understanding.

In addition, don't try to learn every aspect of every financial vehicle in every market in the world. The terminology is massive, because the financial marketplace itself is massive. Start out small and work your way up. The focus of this book is stocks and their corresponding markets. Save learning about the bond market until next week and foreign currency exchanges until the week after that. Eventually it'll all come, you'll see.

CAUTION

Remember that your own money is on the line. If an investment is worth your hard-earned cash, then it's certainly worth taking the time to understand all the information available on your investment.

Finally, and most important, if you don't understand something, either look it up or ask. It is absolutely imperative that when you first learn about the stock market, or the greater financial community, that you fully understand the basics. Subsequent information will grow increasingly complex and most, if not all, of that information will be based on the assumption that you are already familiar with the more basic processes. If you are not, the potential for disaster is greatly increased. Also, even in the more complex processes, ask for clarification of anything you don't understand. Chances are if you don't understand it, others haven't understood it either.

STOCKS ARE ONLY FOR MILLIONAIRES

The belief that stocks are only for millionaires is probably the most common reason why people avoid the stock market. There is a circular train of thought that says that the reason people believe that stocks are only for millionaires is because everyone who buys stocks eventually becomes a millionaire. If only this were true ... the reality, however, is substantially different. This impression is probably based on the numbers bandied about in the financial markets.

- Initial investments in mutual funds currently average $2,500.

- Minimum purchases of municipal bonds can total thousands of dollars.

- A hundred shares of Coca-Cola would cost about $4,400 right now.

Such large amounts are frightening to many people. And, should the average person receive a windfall of $4,400, quite frankly a trip to Disney World would probably precede the purchase of a hundred shares of Coca-Cola.

The irony is that the very people who should be investing in the market are not, for these very reasons, doing so. The investor who can buy a hundred shares of this or that without a second thought is probably so rich that investments are the last thing he or she needs to worry about. On the other hand, the average person on the street—that is, you and I—needs to take a very different approach to investing.

FILL THE BUCKET SLOWLY

This book explains in great detail several strategies for investing minimal amounts on a regular basis. For right now though, consider your beginning investing attempt as filling a bucket under a dripping faucet. The rich person over there is the only person who can afford to pay the water bill this month. As a result, he or she can turn on the faucet and fill up the bucket in a matter of seconds. Since we poorer people can't afford the water bill, we are resigned to filling up our bucket from the drops that are falling from the turned-off, but leaky, faucet. While our method will certainly take more time, in the end it will yield the same results as turning on the faucet. Translate this to money instead of water, and you can see the advantages of constantly dripping small amounts into your investments. In the end, you and the rich person will both have a bucket of water ... make that a bucket of money.

TIP

One fear is that the stock market is geared to big investors and that the average person doesn't have enough funds to actively participate. Deal with this fear by discovering the many investment options that are designed to accommodate people at any financial level.

Like many of the reasons you and other potential investors have for not investing, the concern of not having "enough" money to invest is not new. Fortunately, the financial market is a place of business, and as such it continually modifies itself to attract new investors. Many programs have been created to accommodate new investors having little or no available cash. These are not scams; they are honest attempts to accommodate the situation of the majority of the American public.

Frankly, most people don't have a couple of thousand dollars lying around. So, accommodations exist for people who wish to purchase one share of stock or invest the same amount into a monthly stock purchase. Direct deposit programs can ensure that investment amounts are deducted before the balance is deposited into a checking account. Many brokerage firms periodically reduce the initial amount required to open an account through the use of "sales." Of course you will have to do a little poking around to see what is available out there. As a general rule, however, few companies will refuse your money.

FILL THE BUCKET REGULARLY

The trick to investing with little money is to begin by putting money away regularly. Give the money to a friend or family member, or, better yet, open a savings account and direct deposit some of your paycheck into that account. Put it under your mattress if you need to. When the amount rises to the level of a minimum investment, transfer the money then. Virtually all investments like stock purchases will accept subsequent investments in much smaller amounts (often $50 or $100).

This strategy of small but regular deposits can be really distasteful at first. Once the decision to invest has been made, you, like most investors, will probably want to see progress immediately. Many investors are even disappointed enough by this inertia to abandon their investment careers. But, like the dripping faucet example, the bucket will eventually be filled. Delays in making deposits will only prolong the time needed to fill the bucket.

Finally, be aware that many of these programs and opportunities have, in fact, enticed a number of "average" people to invest in the stock market. Roughly 20 percent of the American population, or 40 million people, currently own stock. And this figure does not even include the people who own stock indirectly through a program such a retirement account. You are not alone in the market, nor are you an inconvenience to those who are already invested. The participation of individual investors is critical to the market's success and, as such, they will be accommodated.

A STOCK MARKET CRASH

Many people are frightened by the stock market because of the stories about past market crashes. Yes, those crashes did happen, but the fear surrounding them is more hype than substance.

TIP

Your fear that the market will collapse as it has done in the past is best dismissed by learning that the probability of another crash is infinitesimal and that the damage caused by previous crashes was not as bad as the public's perception of them.

On October 29, 1929, the Dow, a measurement of the stock market as a whole, fell 30 points to close at 230.07. This represented a drop of almost 13 percent in the whole market. The loss of market value was roughly $14 billion, a staggering sum even now. This meant that $14 billion of the total amount invested into the market by people and by entities such as pension funds was simply gone. The severe ramifications of this event affected even those people who had not actually invested in the market. The subsequent depression, while not directly a result of the stock market crash, further entrenched the idea that investment in the stock market would later reduce the investor to selling apples on a street corner while wearing a barrel. Finally, the stories and depictions of grown men throwing themselves off roofs and crying at their desks assured the general masses that stock investments could only cause heartache.

In addition, 58 years later, the crash of 1929 was surpassed by Black Monday and Black Tuesday on October 19 and 20, 1987, respectively. The Dow's drop of 508 points represented more than a 22 percent drop in the total value of the market and over $500 billion of investor dollars. The crash of '29 was a picnic by comparison.

These events have been highly analyzed, and rational and reasonable explanations for both crashes have been presented and generally accepted by the marketplace. The crash of 1929 was attributed to the market's practice of accepting credit to pay for stock purchases. That practice has long since been cancelled. In addition, program trading, or the ability to trade stocks in a matter of seconds through the use of computers, has been blamed for the crash of 1987. Both of these explanations are probably not particularly important, however, to the people who owned stock at the time of the crashes. The focus is not on why the money was lost, but on the fact that the money was lost.

Two things are important to remember in attempting to place investors' fears in the proper perspective in light of these unfortunate events.

1. The most obvious is that the crashes are infrequent events. Twice since the inception of the stock market in 1792 is not a bad track record. Your chances of being involved in a stock market crash are slim to none. Once invested in the market, you will come to realize that the likelihood of a market crash is so infinitesimal as not to be a concern anywhere in the financial community. By sharing in that confidence, you will be able to discard your fear altogether.

2. Persistent new investors will continually ask, "But what if …?" After all, a chance, no matter how small, of the market's crashing does exist. This question has arisen as a result of the recent collapses of the Asian and Russian markets. It should be pointed out that while markets around the world were crashing, often as a result of the ramifications of prior crashes in other countries, the American market remained stable. The American economy is 16 times larger than its next-largest competitor, a fact that lends an incredible amount of stability and strength to American stock markets. Crashing them simply isn't that easy.

In the highly unlikely case that the markets do fail, remember that in both crashes the average investor may have suffered heavy losses but was not wiped out totally. A loss of 12 to 22 percent of your initial investment is without a doubt disastrous, but it simply isn't that significant when compared with the amount of money that the investment probably had made. In the same train of thought, both of the crashes were preceded by extended favorable, or *bull,* markets.

Happily, the history of the stock market has taught us that bull, or favorable markets tend to last longer than *bear,* or unfavorable, markets. The term "bull" market was taken from early bear trappers. They were notorious for depending on the price of fur to drop so they could purchase pelts cheaply to cover prior options trades they had made. A popular sport at the time, bull and bear baiting, depicted the bull and bear as natural enemies, so the term bull market was used to describe the opposing rising market.

PLAIN ENGLISH

The terms **bull market** and **bear market** are used to describe the conditions of the market. Extended periods when stock prices continue to rise are referred to as bull markets, and periods when stock prices fall are known as bear markets.

In 1929 the stock market had reached a new high of 469.49 the month before the crash. In 1987 the stock market had also reached a new high of 2,722.42, two months before the crash. It is safe to assume, then, that a significant portion of the money being lost by investors was the profits that they had made from their investments. This doesn't mean that their losses weren't real, however. If at the end of the day you still have the money you put into the investment, it is difficult to say you lost anything other than the time that your money was occupied and, of course, any opportunities which were missed as a result of it.

Many fears may be somewhat justified. To not invest because you fear a stock market crash is not one of them.

Is Investing Like Gambling?

Investing in the stock market is not gambling. True, both do attempt to accurately predict future outcomes, but the similarities end there. The inherent fear in gambling is that the outcome is determined by something over which you have no control and understand even less—a pair of dice for example. This is not the case in the stock market. In the stock market, investment decisions are made after a careful analysis of the available information. For example, let us say you receive a windfall of $100.

Option 1: You don't have any real need for that money right now, and you sure wouldn't mind trying to make that money work itself up to a bigger sum. You could place a bet on the roulette wheel, in which case the fate of that $100 would depend entirely on your ability to predict random probability. Regardless of how much research you put into that prediction, the end result once the ball began to roll would be determined by nothing more than sheer chance. That's pretty risky.

Option 2: Investing in stocks works a little differently. Once purchased, a stock represents a partnership between its issuing company and its investor. The investor has agreed to buy into the business and, in return, the issuing company has agreed to try to increase that amount by using it to improve the business. You want the company to succeed; the company wants to succeed. Where is the gamble in that?

Choosing which partnership you want is also not gambling. The research involved here is not an attempt to understand a science like random probability; it is designed to increase familiarity with the company. Think of it like a job interview. During the interviewing process, at one point or another you will be introduced around the office while you take the tour. In this way, you can decide whether this company is one for which you would feel comfortable working. In the same way, information on the issuing companies is made available so you can decide whether this is a company in which you would feel comfortable investing.

TIP

The fear that investing in the stock market is reliant on chance is proved wrong as new investors learn that the processes and tools with which they pick stocks are not based on random chance but on intelligent research and decision making.

The inherent difference between gambling and investing is ultimately control. By gambling your money, you have handed over control of it. The fate of your money rests on something over which you have no control—the hopes that it will manage your money better than you through the magic of probability. By investing, you are charged with the responsibility of learning which stock will best manage your money in a manner consistent with your stated preference. You directly control the company with your vote, and you can revoke your partnership at any time. Because you are appropriately informed, the decisions are not left to chance.

IT WILL TAKE TOO MUCH TIME

Initializing and subsequently diversifying your *portfolio* should never take up an inordinate amount of your time. Even as you expand your portfolio and begin to include other financial instruments, a process known as *diversification,* the initial purchase of stock will be your decision. Should you decide to spend hours researching, you are perfectly free to do so. Or, you might ask a friend to give you advice. You decide to purchase the stock for whatever reason you consider important. Research is never required.

PLAIN ENGLISH

A **portfolio** is a collective term for all your investments. It should consist of cash as well as different kinds of investments, such as stocks and bonds. Determining how much of each you want is a process known as **diversification.**

After purchasing the stock, even monitoring its performance is optional. Should you decide you want to know the stock's performance for the day, through the use of several methods described in this book, you will be able to uncover any information in a matter of seconds. But most important, you still control the amount of time you allot to monitoring your stock's performance. Monitoring your investments is also not required.

So the total time commitment is solely your decision. That doesn't mean you shouldn't take the time to learn anything. You obviously have some interest in the stock market, or you wouldn't want to invest in it. As with other areas that catch your attention, you should take some time to learn more and to become increasingly familiar with the market.

What inevitably happens is you start to become interested. Once you've learned how stocks work, you start to wonder how bonds work. In addition to stocks you already own, you begin to check the daily performance of stocks that you are considering purchasing. After learning the business of one company, you become interested in how the competition is being run. As your interest in finance expands, it is highly possible that you may find yourself putting more time into it. However, this is your choice. The reverse is also true: Should you have no interest in your investments or later lose interest, you are free to ignore the whole lot.

TIP

The fear that managing your portfolio will consume too much time is dismissed when new investors discover that research is available but not necessary and that they control the amount of time they want to devote to research.

As your holdings grow and expand, the amount of time you dedicate to learning about new investment vehicles and to monitoring your expanded portfolio will also grow, but only infinitesimally since the entire process requires only a few seconds in the first place. You could continue to invest in the vehicles with which you are already familiar and thereby further reduce additional time commitments. Or, you can begin to learn about alternative investments at your leisure.

Like any commitment you make, investing will take up some time, but how much depends on your decision. The truth, however, is that by the time you have so many stocks that maintaining them is actually causing you time problems, you should be rich enough to afford to pay people to do that for you.

THE 30-SECOND RECAP

- Financial terminology should not be intimidating.

- The basics of the stock market are not complicated.

- Investment options exist for people of any income level.

- The market is a safe stable place to put your money.

- The stock market is not a game of chance.

- The time required to manage your investments is minimal.

Lesson 2

Why You Should Invest in Stocks

In this lesson you will learn about the advantages stocks have over other investment vehicles.

Stocks Rock!

There is no shortage of things in which to invest your money. So why choose stocks? Quite simply, because stocks are your best bet. Since its inception, the stock market has consistently delivered the best overall returns when compared with the returns of investments like real estate. Since the purpose of investing is to watch your money grow, the logical choice is to place your money where it has the best chance of doing that.

> **TIP**
>
> Many of the skills you will learn to determine whether stocks are the appropriate investment vehicle for you will later be the same skills you will use to select stocks—you will be able to compare stocks' returns, assets, and liabilities with other available investment options, for example.

There are, however, mitigating circumstances and characteristics that may make other investment vehicles seem attractive as well. Other investment vehicles you might consider are …

- Bonds
- Cash
- Mutual funds

When comparing or considering these vehicles as investment options, be aware that as their methods of producing returns differ, so, too, do the individual risks associated with each vehicle.

STOCKS VS. BONDS

Stocks and bonds go together like peanut butter and jelly or macaroni and cheese. This is meant to imply that to a certain extent you should buy some bonds. But, if you are trying to decide between purchasing a share of stock or purchasing a bond, you should probably go with the stock. The return for stock averages about 12 percent, whereas the average return on a bond is only 5 to 6 percent. The following table illustrates the approximate annual returns by asset class since 1926. The overall average inflation rate has also been provided as a reference upon which to base their profitability.

Asset Class	Average Annual Return
Small cap stock	12.4%
Large cap stock	10.3%
Corporate bonds	5.6%
Government bonds	5.0%
Treasury bills	3.7%
Inflation	3.1%

Please be aware that the "no limit" policy on a stock's growth is a Catch-22. Because no limit is placed on how large the investment can grow, no limit can likewise be placed on how small the investment may shrink. As a result, the single biggest factor that makes a bond a more desirable investment is its guarantee of capital preservation. This means that when lending your money to a company through the purchase of a bond, you may make less profit, but you are assured of getting back at least the original amount you paid to purchase the bond. Stocks make no such guarantee.

CAUTION

Stocks have the potential to provide higher returns than bonds; however, bonds offer a higher degree of security for the principal amount invested.

In the very unlikely case that the issuing company of either a stock or a bond should go out of business, all bond holders would be paid first from the liquidation of the company's remaining assets. This gives bondholders a minimal edge over stockholders in recovering their initial investment.

Remember, however, that the most fundamental reason for any investment is to make money. By providing an investment with the necessary flexibility to make larger gains, it becomes capable of making equally large losses. This concept is known as "risk and reward."

With stock it is possible to get the best of both worlds: the safety of bonds with the profit potential of stocks. Investments in solid companies, such as IBM or McDonald's for example, carry little if any practical risk of going defunct anytime soon.

STOCKS VS. CASH

Cash, in financial terms, refers to any type of investment that is extremely liquid. A money market account, for example, is considered cash because the account holder can withdraw his or her money with relative ease, including drawing on the account with a personal check. Cash can also refer to the money in your checking and savings accounts or the money hidden under your mattress.

TIP

Investing in stocks will almost definitely provide a higher return than allowing your money to remain in cash or investing it in a cash investment. However, cash has a degree of liquidity not offered by stock.

The biggest problem with a cash type of "investment" is that it really isn't much of an investment. Putting your money under your mattress is not going to produce a dime regardless of how long you leave it under there. Checking and savings accounts are certainly necessary accounts to have these days, and they are excellent for what they are; but they are not investments, nor are they geared to behave as such. Any profit-making ability they may have, such as interest-bearing checking, will be absolutely minimal.

The least-offensive cash investment is the money market account. The *money market account* combines the best aspects of cash investments and mutual funds to create a hybrid that provides a higher return than anything you could get from your mattress or checking account, yet it keeps your money absolutely safe. Fortunately, stock and cash are not rivals for your money. They each carry very specific and different functions, so you can easily and quickly decide where your money should go. An investment should always be made with money you can afford to lose. If you need that money, it should stay in cash. Almost anyone involved in finance will agree that a person needs to have three to six months worth of living expenses in cash before considering any investment.

PLAIN ENGLISH

> A **money market fund** is a mutual fund that purchases absolutely safe investment such as treasury bills backed by the full faith of the U.S. Government.

What it boils down to is this: First make sure you have sufficient cash on hand for any emergency. Cash accounts, used this way, should take priority over investing in stock. Once you have collected what you consider to be sufficient cash, however, don't let future income just laze around in your cash accounts; put it to work in the stock market.

STOCKS VS. MUTUAL FUNDS

The recent rise in the popularity of *mutual funds* has brought them under wider and more substantial scrutiny. Many people are discovering that mutual funds are an excellent investment option, but stocks are still better.

PLAIN ENGLISH

A **mutual fund** is a mass portfolio that has been collected by a mutual fund manager and is professionally managed for its owners or shareholders.

A mutual fund can be composed of any combination of investments, or it can focus on only one investment vehicle—stocks, for example. In fact, the vast majority of mutual funds are totally composed of stocks, or at least contain some stocks in their composition. It would appear, then, that investing in a mutual fund composed of stocks would differ only slightly from investing in the stocks themselves.

To some extent, this is true. But because mutual funds come as a package deal, there are substantial differences between the two as investments.

First, you lose a lot of control over the mix of your investments. When you purchase a share of a mutual fund, you purchase a portion of each of the stocks in the fund. You cannot sell off any stock in the mix with which you are not comfortable, nor can you add stock that you think might be a valuable asset to the fund. Of course, you could always buy that stock on your own, but then you would be purchasing stock instead of mutual funds. The ability to select stock individually has become particularly important with the advent of *social investing*. Staunch environmentalists, for example, may wish to purchase stock only in those companies that are environmentally friendly. This might prove difficult to achieve with the broad number of securities within a mutual fund.

PLAIN ENGLISH

Social investing is a relatively new concept whereby factors such as the nature of a company's product or service and its reputation for diversity and ecological responsibility come into play when determining whether its stock is a worthy investment.

In addition, theoretically you could never make the same amount of money with a mutual fund that you could if you purchased the stock contained in the mutual fund's mix directly. This is because a portion (albeit a small portion) of the money you spend to purchase a share of the mutual fund is used to pay the people who manage the fund, rent the building, and otherwise cover any expenses associated with maintaining the fund. These same charges wouldn't apply if you purchased the stock directly. I said "theoretically" because the broker fees you would pay to purchase shares of all those stocks would probably quickly overtake any management fees you would pay to a corresponding mutual fund.

TIP

Stocks by default provide higher returns than mutual funds since management fees are not levied on stock owners. Mutual funds, however, offer a higher degree of diversification.

For that reason, mutual funds, like bonds and cash, do have a place in the investment arena. By purchasing a share of a mutual fund, you as an individual investor can place your money in much the same circumstances as the money of a large investor. By investing in a mutual fund, you can spread a minor investment over several stocks, thereby diversifying your holdings and mitigating risk. At some point, however, the safety of the mutual funds will become constraints that will eventually make you move on to purchasing individual stocks.

The 30-Second Recap

- Different investment vehicles carry risks particular to them and may complicate comparison to stocks.

- Stocks provide the highest returns over cash investments but cash investments are the most secure.

- Stocks historically provide higher returns than bonds but investment in bonds is more secure.

- Stocks can provide higher returns than mutual funds but lack their diversification.

- As an investment's ability to produce higher gains grows, so, too, does the risk of losing your money.

LESSON 3

How Much Do You Have to Invest?

In this lesson you will learn where investing fits into your total financial picture and how to determine how much money you have to invest.

DETERMINING YOUR OVERALL FINANCIAL PICTURE

Investments can be a very important part of your overall financial management. In order for your investments to be good financial management decisions, it is important that you have a very clear picture of how much money you have and how much of it can be invested. This is not an arbitrary decision, but one that should be made after considering several factors including those discussed here. Failure to earmark your money in advance could prove disastrous, because without a monetary plan you may find yourself inappropriately allocating money to the wrong purpose. Again, investments are only one portion of a good financial management plan that should also include

- Determining income

- Determining expenses

- Amassing savings

- Paying down debt

- Reviewing your credit report/establishing credit

Think of your plan as a budget. Although the word *budget* in itself is distasteful to many people, a budget can be used to make life a lot easier, rather than more constrained. A budget is nothing more than determining how much available money you have and the total of all your financial commitments. By knowing this information in advance, you can decide how much of your available cash you wish to allocate to savings, expenses, and debt. Doing this ahead of time will make your life easier since no unpleasant surprises will arise later on that you must handle. Once you've decided how to allot your money, you can determine how much of your disposable income is available for investing. Again, by planning ahead, you avoid placing yourself in uncomfortable financial circumstances later on.

SUFFICIENT SAVINGS

Before allocating money for investing, your first and most important task is to ensure that you have amassed *sufficient savings* to see you through any emergency. An amount equal to three to six months' living expenses is the general rule. Setting aside this sum is absolutely essential, because once an investment is made, it should be left alone to work its magic and increase its value. Like checking a cake while it is baking, repeatedly withdrawing and redepositing stock investments will all but negate their progress.

In addition, this savings amount should be readily available. This means that you should be able to quickly get your hands on that money in cash. In the event of an emergency, time is rarely available to accommodate the paperwork or functions necessary to get your money out of the stock market. This statement is not meant to frighten you into thinking that getting your money out of the market is a long, laborious process—because it isn't. However, getting your money may take a couple of days, or even several weeks, depending on the arrangements you make. In an emergency, you can't wait that long to get your cash; you need to be able to go to an ATM machine and get your hands on it immediately.

PLAIN ENGLISH

> **Sufficient savings** means the amount of readily accessible money or credit that you would need in case of an unforeseen emergency. This money, usually three to six months' worth of expenses, should be kept in an easily accessible account, and collecting it should precede any investments.

If you don't currently have sufficient savings for an emergency fund, forget about investing for right now. Your first priority is to amass your safety net by beginning to put away some amount into this fund regularly. In addition, any unexpected windfalls should also go directly into this fund.

If you have not previously had a fund of this type, it may be tempting to use that money as it starts to grow. By raiding your fund, however, you are only further postponing the time when you will be able to invest. You must have sufficient savings before investing. The importance of this fund cannot be stressed enough. It is, without a doubt, more important than the ability to invest.

AMASSING YOUR EMERGENCY FUND

Having stressed the importance of sufficient savings, a couple of tricks may help you amass this amount a little more quickly. Instead of actually maintaining six months' worth of living expenses—which to anyone would be a substantial amount—remember that the purpose of this fund is to be able to deal with any emergency immediately. For that reason, available credit may be substituted for actual cash as long as the credit is backed up by other cash.

Thus, if you have, say, $10,000 in the fund, you may not necessarily want to keep all that money in a savings account. Let's say that you have a credit card with a $5,000 limit. You could invest $5,000 of the $10,000 in something that is absolutely safe, such as a CD (certificate of deposit) or money market fund. In case of emergency, the credit card would substitute for that $5,000 until you could get the cash out in a couple of days. Once you received the cash, you would apply it to whatever amount you had put on the credit card, paying off that debt. The advantage of this plan is that you haven't sacrificed your cash availability and at the same time your $5,000 has earned more than it would have sitting in a savings account.

Getting Rid of Debt

The only possible problem with the preceding tip would be failing to pay off the credit card immediately upon receipt of the $5,000. With interest rates on credit cards currently hovering around 20 percent, any profits made from the investment of that $5,000 would quickly disappear if you had to pay interest on a credit card debt. In much the same way, carrying any type of debt can wipe out profits made by investments.

For example, it would make little sense to invest a windfall of cash into a stock with a 12-percent return if you were simultaneously carrying the same amount of credit card debt at a 20-percent interest rate. The profits being generated by your investment would disappear when paying the interest charges on your credit card. In this case, it would probably be a better idea to use that money to pay off the credit card first.

CAUTION

Make sure that the profits you are making from your investments are not being used to pay higher interest rates on debt you are currently carrying. Determine where your money is best applied.

This rule about paying off debt before you start to invest is not absolute, however. Many debts, such as a mortgage or a student loan, for example, could not be realistically paid off in a relatively short amount of time. And postponing your investing until this type of debt is paid off would be a bad idea. What is important, then, is to consider where the money could best be put to use. If you have only $100 to invest and you are carrying a mortgage or a student loan of $30,000, applying the $100 to such a large amount would make no noticeable impact. If you used the $100 to purchase a share of stock, however, the money would probably grow substantially during the time it took you to pay off the loan. In this case, it might be a better decision to invest the money rather than attempt to pay off a debt.

Each situation will prove unique and must be evaluated on its own terms. In the scenario just given, for example, the stock may not be making as much in profits as the interest charges being applied to the loan. Nonetheless, since the $100 amount would not affect the interest amount, the amount earned by the stock is at least somewhat offsetting the amount being paid out for interest. In addition, a certain amount of debt is a good thing for credit ratings and for learning money management.

Debt a good thing? Sure. Most entities that issue credit, such as mortgage companies and credit or charge cards, base a substantial amount of their decision to offer credit to you on previous creditors' reports. These reports are amassed by three companies—TRW, Equifax, and Experian—that provide them, upon request, to the companies that are considering offering you credit. Should you not have any debt, your credit record would be minimal, if it exists at all. Each of these companies will also furnish you one copy of your current credit report annually free upon request. Contact information for these companies is provided in Appendix B, "Resources."

What is important to remember is that your finances are not contained in individual silos but rather are fully integrated and must thus be considered as a whole. To be perfectly frank, investing in stocks requires a certain amount of maturity and the ability to effectively handle finances. Neither one of these characteristics is often found in a person who is carrying an excessive amount of debt.

DETERMINING YOUR EXPENSES

There are several reasons why it is of particular importance to *determine your expenses* when attempting to calculate how much disposable cash you have for investment. The most obvious reason is that you need to keep enough money to pay your bills.

> **PLAIN ENGLISH**
>
> It may seem obvious, but **determining your expenses** is the process of realistically determining how much of your income is currently spoken for in providing for your day-to-day expenses. Establishing this amount should precede any investing.

Another reason for figuring out your expenses is that you will gain a clearer understanding of your own present financial health. You will quickly realize how much of your money you are spending and where and on what you are spending it. Armed with this knowledge, you are in a much better position to make investments relative to your overall financial picture.

For example, you may realize that you are spending excessive amounts in one particular area and you may decide to try to cut back a little there to free up some cash. This newly available cash could be used to invest in stocks. However, the amount invested wouldn't even be available had you not determined your expenses and then subsequently noticed that one expense area was particularly high. So, determining your expenses in advance was directly responsible for your ability to make that investment.

The last reason for determining your expenses is simply good financial management, which includes getting rid of debt and acquiring sufficient savings to deal with any emergency. Good financial management is the basis for effective stock investing. You need to be able to effectively manage your daily finances before venturing into the more complicated world of investment.

Paper Investing

Having confronted your fears and determined how much you have available to invest, you are almost ready to begin your career as an investor. However, since money is involved, it's not a bad idea to first try a dry run and apply the information you learn here to a fictitious portfolio of stocks.

This process, better known as *paper investing,* is a particularly good method for getting started in investing. Through paper investing, you as a potential investor can in absolute safety apply your new knowledge to real-life scenarios, later discovering whether your decisions were correct.

Use the knowledge you gain in this book to decide upon your standards for selecting an investment strategy, choosing stocks, and achieving a portfolio mix. Write these particulars down; then pick investments or stocks that meet all, or at least most of, your stated criteria. Monitor these investments over a period of time (a couple of weeks or months) to see if your initial decision remains a good one.

TIP

Amassing a fictitious portfolio, or **paper investing,** based on information you have learned is a good idea for new investors. Analyze your portfolio's performance to determine how good your initial investment decision was.

You can begin your paper investing now, and increase your selections as you continue to learn new and relevant information throughout the book. Paper investing will make you more comfortable with the real investment process and will provide real-life examples to illustrate many of the theories presented here. Both of these actions will increase your understanding and comfort level and make you a better investor.

THE 30-SECOND RECAP

- Investments are only one part of responsible financial management.

- Before investing, you should have savings of three to six months of living expenses.

- Lower or get rid of debt. The interest you pay on it may negate any profits you make from your investments.

- Determine your income and expenses so that you can appropriately allocate your money.

- Before investing, try a dry run by charting imaginary investments' performances.

LESSON 4
What Is a Stock?

In this lesson you will learn what defines a stock, how stocks operate, and how to differentiate among the various types of stock.

STOCK TALK

A *stock* is a proportional ownership interest in a company. Or, in simplest terms, a stock is a portion of the value of a company. When you buy stock in a company, you are actually purchasing a piece of that company.

For example, let's say that we added up all of Widget Inc.'s assets, or the things that Widget Inc. owns—computers, office buildings, etc.— and the value of everything came to $1,000.00. Then let's say for argument's sake that Widget Inc. issues 1,000 shares of stock for people to buy. If you buy one share of Widget Inc., you own 1/1,000 of everything that Widget Inc. owns.

PLAIN ENGLISH

A **stock** is a means by which the average person can purchase a company by dividing its purchase price into shares small enough to be accessibly priced for everyone.

You are actually an owner of the world-famous Widget Inc. company, and, as such, you get all the rights and responsibilities that go along with being an owner. When the management of Widget Inc. makes decisions regarding the company, like buying a new building, they need to get your approval—yours and the other 999 people's, assuming each bought one share like you. If you buy two shares you own twice as much of the company and have twice as many votes in decisions on how it will be run. While the company's board of directors will deal with most day-to-day issues, it is your vote which places them or removes them from the board, thereby making you the ultimate authority. You can go to the company's annual meeting and cast your vote, or you can vote by absentee ballot. The absentee ballot is called a *proxy;* it is a legal form by which an investor votes in absentia, transferring his or her voting authority to another party.

PLAIN ENGLISH

A **proxy** is the ballot form that is sent to shareholders for their votes. Since few people actually attend annual meetings, the word "proxy" has become synonymous with the vote itself. Most people refer to "voting their proxy."

The rights and responsibilities of owning stock, as discussed earlier, both apply to a proxy in that voting on how the company operates is a right reserved exclusively for stockholders. It is also your responsibility, however, in that by not voting, you are leaving the management of "your" company in the hands of others.

DIVIDENDS

When the company makes money, so do you—if you are a shareholder. The portion of a corporation's after-tax earnings that is distributed to stockholders is called a *dividend.* Companies can certainly lose money too, in which case there would be no dividends. You would not, however, have to pay out any money, although the value of the stock would drop as any company that is losing money is obviously less valuable.

TIP

> When the company makes a profit, the whole profit, or some of it, is divided up among everyone who has a share. These payments are called **dividends** (divide up—dividends, get it?). Try to buy stock in a company that will continue to make a profit.

ASSETS

Anything you own that's valuable is an asset.

WHAT'S A COMPANY WORTH?

Determining the value of a company is a little different from valuing tangible goods like cars and houses. In both cases, you would list the real value of the components and the real value of the liabilities, add the whole thing together, and the end sum would be the value of the company.

For example, at Widget Inc. you could determine that the current stock of widgets is worth $100, the office equipment and supplies are worth $100, and the building Widget Inc. owns is worth $100. In addition, Widget Inc. owes its suppliers $50 and still has an outstanding mortgage of $50, so you would subtract that $100 total and the end result of $200 would be Widget Inc.'s value or *net worth*.

It gets a little more complicated than that, as the real value of a company is often in things that are less tangible, name recognition, for example. Most people will buy Coca-Cola before they buy generic soda, so there's actually value in owning the name Coca-Cola. The name itself sells cans of soda. That's an edge that Coca-Cola has on the generic competition. Unfortunately, that edge can't be documented on anything like a balance sheet. That edge is one of Coca-Cola's *assets,* and it makes Coca-Cola a more valuable company.

Companies are often valued not at what they currently are, but at what they are capable of becoming. This is called *growth potential*. For example, let's say yours is the only company in America that makes Widgets from plastic; all the other companies make theirs from apples. This year, there's a huge freeze and all the apple crops are lost. Since your little Widget company is about to become the only company who can still produce Widgets, its value will go through the roof even if at this moment you haven't actually changed a thing.

PLAIN ENGLISH

An **asset** is an item on a balance sheet that shows the book value of something owned. Anything you own that's valuable is an asset.

On the other side are those things that detract from a company's value, known as *liabilities*. A liability can include anything such as outstanding debt, an inferior market share or position, or a bad reputation. While a debt can certainly make its way onto the company's balance sheet, again, the more intangible items such as a bad reputation or recent news events won't be listed.

The biggest complication, however, is that you can't really put a price tag on these types of things (what exactly is a good reputation worth? how much does a bad reputation hurt a company's sales?), so stocks are actually worth only what people think they are worth. Or, in other words, stocks are worth what people are willing to pay for them.

If you are willing to paint someone's house for $40, and someone is willing to pay you $40 to do it, that's exactly what your service is worth. If you want $50 but can't find anyone to pay that, then the service may not be worth $50. And the reverse is true too. If you agree to $40, not knowing that someone would be willing to pay you $50, then the service is actually worth $50 and you have just undersold yourself. In economic terms, this phenomenon is called *supply and demand*. It's what drives the stock market and determines the prices of all stocks.

KINDS OF STOCK

The stocks themselves get a little more complicated than the paint job scenario just mentioned. There are different kinds of stock, and they are differentiated by some very fine print. While all stocks represent ownership of shares of a company, they aren't all alike. A stock can be an actual document or a virtual notation on someone's computer. Here is a list of stock categories:

- **Blue Chip Stock.** A share of one of the most established and financially secure companies in the country.

- **Secondary Stock.** A share of a company with substantial backing that is not quite considered blue chip.

- **Income Stock.** A stock that is usually characterized by its issuing company's focus on providing higher dividends.

- **Growth Stock.** The stock of a company that is still small but is believed by its shareholders to have great growth potential.

- **Penny Stock.** A highly speculative stock in a company with little or no real value other than its uncertain growth potential.

THE TWO MAIN ISSUES OF STOCK

In addition to the unofficial kinds of stocks just discussed, the market has two issues of stock to accommodate different types of investors: common stock and preferred stock. As a very general rule, the benefits of common stock tend to be more geared for individual investors while those of preferred stock tend to be more geared to the needs of institutional investors such as pension funds, mutual funds, and banks.

COMMON STOCK

Aptly named, *common stock* is the one most people think of when they hear the word *stock*. It's also the kind of stock most widely bought and sold, or in investor lingo—traded. It represents basic ownership of part of a company, as was described in the beginning of this lesson. The owner of one share of common stock gets one vote, or one proxy, on company matters. As stated earlier, two shares equals two votes and so on.

When the value of the company goes up as it did in the example of the apple crop freeze, share owners make money because the value of the company has increased and subsequently the stock has gone up also. This is called *capital gain.*

When discussing types of investments, you will often hear terms such as financial "instruments" and "vehicles." These terms are not "financial terms" which imply anything significant but simply words which are used interchangeably instead of less professional-sounding terms such as "things" or "stuff."

PLAIN ENGLISH

Capital is the original amount you invested in your financial instrument. A capital gain is an appreciation of the value of the financial instrument, such as a stock, in which the initial principal was invested. If your stock is worth more now than what you paid for it, then you have realized a capital gain.

If you had bought stock in one of those companies that makes Widgets from apples, the value of your company and subsequently its stock would have decreased because of the deep freeze that destroyed the apple crop. You would have suffered what's called a *capital loss.*

Capital gains and losses are one of the two ways stock make and lose money (the other being dividends). In addition, however, other factors such as the taxes on capital gains should always be taken into consideration. Current capital gains taxes are so high as to often negate much of a stock's potential earnings and make many stocks unattractive to investors for that reason. As with any investment, you always run the risk of losing the initial money you invested (capital loss). While in such a case it would offer little if any consolation, you would, at least, receive a tax credit for the money you lost.

When the Widget company makes money by selling all those Widgets, the owners of the stock get a proportional cut of the profits in the form of a dividend. The investor has the choice to take the dividend as a payment after paying taxes on the profit, or reinvesting it to buy more stock. Dividends are related to capital gains in that any company which is consistently making profits and paying them out in dividends will soon be discovered as a great company. For that reason, the value of the company would eventually rise and create a capital gain for its owner when he or she sells the stock.

PREFERRED STOCK

Preferred stock is different from common stock in that preferred stock owners get their dividend payments before the common stock owners. Also, should the company go out of business, preferred stock owners get paid their share of whatever's left before the owners of common stock get paid.

So why isn't everyone buying preferred stock? First, companies don't issue preferred stock until after common stock has been issued, so there's less of it. Second, preferred stock owners don't generally get proxy rights. Third and most important, preferred stock owners usually get paid a preset dividend regardless of how much money the company makes.

Further confusing things, companies can issue any number of different preferred stocks, or *classes*. Usually, the different kinds are labeled *A, B, C,* etc., and each class can have a different price or dividend. These classes are highly flexible regarding their similarities and/or differences to each other. This flexibility is necessary to accommodate the circumstances of the issuing company at the time. For that reason, it would be difficult if not impossible to provide a complete listing of preferred stock classes anywhere. As always, the responsibility of discovering the nuances of each class is left up to the investor.

THE 30-SECOND RECAP

- A stock represents a proportional ownership of a company.

- Stocks make money when the company makes a profit and splits it among the stockholders (known as a dividend) or when the actual value of the company goes up (known as a capital gain).

- Valuing a company is the sum of its assets and liabilities; this is also known as its *net worth.*

- Stocks are split into two issues—common stock that appeals more to individual investors; and the various classes of preferred stock that are geared more to the needs of institutional investors.

- Various terms have arisen to describe the different behaviors of stock including blue chip, secondary, income, growth, and penny stocks.

LESSON 5

The Five Types of Stock

In this lesson you will learn how the goals of stock and the conditions of their issuing companies are described using Wall Street terms.

STOCK CHARACTERISTICS

Companies, like almost anything else, are available for purchase and sale. Your daily newspaper certainly covers the more noteworthy purchases such as AOL's recent purchase of Time Warner. In addition, however, and on a much smaller scale, individuals can purchase a franchise restaurant like McDonald's, a small bed and breakfast, or the local corner store. Even professional practices such as a dentistry or professional massage parlor are usually sold when the proprietor retires or leaves the profession. As these businesses vary, so does the accompanying stock. Over the years, investors have come up with descriptive names to characterize the differences between these stocks.

This is not meant to imply that all stocks bear little resemblance to each other. In fact, stocks actually tend to be more similar in most aspects. For example, all horses are basically the same—four legs, one mane, and so on. A race horse, however, varies from a plow horse primarily because of what the owner expects from it, namely a race horse will try to win races and a plow horse will pull a plow. As a result, the horses would differ in what they would be fed, what kinds of ailments would be more common to each, and how they would be treated.

So, too, most stocks have particular aims that define them. One stock may attempt to provide higher dividends, while another may focus on higher capital gains, and yet another may focus on raising quick money for the issuing company immediately. Due to these differing focuses, companies will treat their stocks accordingly in order to maximize the stock's ability to meet their goals.

Goals are usually determined when a stock is first issued by the company in what is known as an *initial public offering*. This is nothing more than a descriptive name for the first time a stock is available for sale. It is also known as a company "going public," which, as the name implies, means that portions of the company, or shares of stock, are now available for the public to purchase. The decision to "go public" and what the aims of the stock will be are pretty much determined by the board of directors or whoever the owner of the business was before it went public. Let me point out that these decisions are fluid and please note that many companies do not go public at all. Many are owned by a person or a family that keeps them in tight control. No company is ever required to go public.

You, as an investor, have the responsibility to determine what use you want to make of the stock, your goal in purchasing the stock, and which kind of stock would most likely fulfill your goal.

The following classifications are not official and are not determined by any governing body. They are also not set in stone—what is considered an income stock to one may be considered a penny stock to another. Like many industry terms, these are fluid, intended to cover as many angles as possible. For example, when gambling, no set size bet actually constitutes a high roller. What constitutes a fortune to one person is but a drop in the hat to the next. So too, these terms are not meant to imply anything definitive, but rather to be used as an aid when discussing and studying stock.

BLUE CHIP STOCKS

Blue chip stocks are stocks in companies that historically have exhibited unparalleled and unquestionable strength; such companies are the stalwarts of American business. Stocks of this type include companies such as IBM, AT&T, and General Motors. These are the stocks whose long-term success is guaranteed. These are not stocks in any one particular industry, computers for example, but rather the most stable and solid stocks on the market regardless of the products they produce or services they offer. The focus here is on the behavior of the stock.

For example, IBM and General Motors produce vastly different products but, regardless of their production, the stocks of both are very stable as the companies are such behemoths that very little can cause their corresponding stock to fluctuate much. As a general rule, these companies tend to have been in business a very long time, although Intel, for example, is considered a blue chip stock and has been in business a short time, relatively speaking.

Blue chips almost guarantee that novice investors will not lose money while enabling them to learn and practice their investment strategies with real stock. In addition, blue chip profits are based on investors purchasing the stock and holding on to it for an extended period of time, a highly desirable strategy for novice investors.

SECONDARY STOCKS

Secondary stocks are still up there in investor confidence—they simply are not in the blue chip league. The easiest distinction of this is through a complicated financial area known as market capitalization by which financiers determine how much money would be required to bring such a company to the market today. This is often determined by what the company actually came to the market with, regardless of when it happened. Suffice it to say for our purposes that stocks of this type still include well-established companies such as BancOne (finance), Teledyne (technology), and Best Foods (food service). Even though the chances are slim that these companies will go out of business, secondary stocks do tend to be a little more volatile— meaning the price fluctuates more—than blue chip stock. This could be due to any number of reasons, not the least being that these companies as a general rule are smaller than blue chips and/or do not have as established a reputation.

PLAIN ENGLISH

Secondary stocks are shares of companies that have been brought to the market with a significant amount of investor's money. The amount of money is known as "market capitalization." The market capitalization is quite large, but still less than that of companies whose stock is considered blue chip.

INCOME STOCKS

Income stocks are stocks in companies that are usually fairly well established and that make a relatively regular amount of profit. Income stocks generally have a solid history of making regular dividend payments. This does not mean that these companies *never* reinvest their profits; however, providing dividends is more important, so reinvestment will usually be a small percentage of the profit if it exists at all. Investors will usually buy this type of stock because they wish to receive regular dividend payments. As a result of all this regularity, there's usually very little volatility involved in the value of these stocks. Examples of these types of stock include Bell Atlantic (communications), Con-Ed (utilities) and General Electric (utilities). As you can see from these examples, these industries tend to receive regular payments from their customers as opposed to industries such as retail stores where income could vary significantly.

PLAIN ENGLISH

Income stocks are stocks that are usually characterized by the issuing company's focus on providing higher dividends as opposed to reinvesting its profits in further growing the business to provide capital gains.

GROWTH STOCKS

Growth stocks are stocks that are being valued on their potential, as in the Widget company/apple freeze example in Lesson 4, "What Is a

Stock?" Investors usually bet that the companies will become successful as a result of a great product or service or capable management
rather than something as dramatic and unpredictable as a crop frost.
Growth stocks typically put all the profits they make back into growing the business, so investors buy this stock because they believe the
value of the stock will go up as opposed to buying the stock for the
purpose of receiving regular or substantial dividend payments. Companies with this type of stock include EMC (computer technology),
AOL (Internet service provider), and Wal-Mart (retail sales). Investors
who purchase this type of stock usually plan to make their profits by
selling the stock for more than they bought it for. It is important then
to push growth stock of those companies you believe will ultimately
prove successful.

TIP

> Because growth stocks also best operate on the strat-
> egy of buy and hold, these too are an excellent stock
> for novice investors to consider. Be aware, however,
> that as growth stocks have (and plan) to grow con-
> siderably faster than blue chip stocks, so too do the
> opportunities for loss.

PENNY STOCKS

Penny stocks are stocks for the high rollers, because they usually don't
have much that is substantial to offer investors other than their potential. Penny stock investors are usually investors who are hoping to buy
the stock before the rest of the world catches on to what a great deal
it's going to become. Penny stock prices are, for that very reason,
extremely volatile. Examples of penny stocks are difficult to name, as
quite frankly few stick around long enough to be of any notice. If you
are absolutely determined to find some, look at the "Over the Counter" listing in *The Wall Street Journal.* Any stocks priced under $10
per share are considered penny stocks.

Please notice that no examples were provided in the description of penny stocks. This is because penny stocks make themselves highly attractive to new investors through their lower prices (generally under $10). As a result, newer investors often purchase these stocks without considering the fact that (quite frankly) most people lose whatever money they have invested.

Stock Class Quick Reference

Stock Type	Example 1	Example 2	Example 3
Blue chip	IBM	GM	AT&T
Secondary	Teledyne	BancOne	Best Foods
Income	Bell Atlantic	General Electric	Con-Ed(ison)
Growth	Wal-Mart	AOL	EMC
Penny	Somanetics Corp.	Explorer Technologies, Inc.	Amistar Corp.

THE 30-SECOND RECAP

- Blue chip stocks are the most stable of all stocks in price fluctuation.

- Secondary stocks are also high in investor confidence but are differentiated from blue chips in that they have a lower market capitalization.

- Income stocks are those whose primary focus is to provide regular and higher dividend payments.

- Growth stocks are stocks that pay little if any dividends, choosing instead to increase capital gains by reinvesting profits to grow the business.

- Penny stocks are characterized by their low prices and extreme price fluctuations, best avoided by novice investors.

LESSON 6
Stock Derivatives

In this lesson you will learn about several methods people use to make profits from stock outside of capital gains and dividends.

WHAT ARE DERIVATIVES?

People are constantly coming up with new and more amazing ways to make (and lose) money, and the world of stocks is no exception. In addition to proper stock as discussed in Lessons 4, "What Is a Stock?" and 5, "The Five Types of Stock," a number of other stock-like products have appeared in which people speculate and invest. These products, while not exactly stocks, are directly based on stocks or are otherwise traded in stock markets. Or, they are derived from stocks. Because of these characteristics, such products are often referred to as *derivatives* (derived from—derivatives, get it?). Here are the various types of derivatives:

- Subscription rights

- Warrants

- Options

- Calls

- Puts

- Stock index options

Since derivatives generally require more expertise and are substantially more volatile than simple stock transactions, newer investors often avoid them. These same characteristics, however, are the main reasons why derivatives are particularly popular both with seasoned experts having substantial sums and with adventurous new investors who have yet to grow their portfolios.

SUBSCRIPTION RIGHTS

Subscription rights are formalized promises from a company to sell its stock to its current stockholders at a price reduced from the market price in the event of new stock being issued.

> **PLAIN ENGLISH**
>
> **Subscription rights** are a type of financial instrument that a company grants to its current shareholders, giving them the option to buy future issues of company stock at a discount price.

For example, let's say you own 100 shares of XYZ Company for which you paid $8 per share. XYZ Company issued only 200 shares to begin with, so you effectively bought and own half of XYZ Company. Now the price of XYZ Company has risen to $10 per share, and XYZ Company decides that it wants to raise some more cash to open a new Widget factory in a nearby town. So, the company offers another 200 shares of stock for sale. Your half-ownership of XYZ Company has been effectively cut to one-fourth with the stroke of a pen. "That's not fair," you cry. "I bought those 100 shares initially so that I could have half-ownership in the company."

XYZ Company certainly doesn't want to cause hard feelings in those people who already own its stock, because a sell-off by angry shareholders could lower the price of the stock, and the company would thereby effectively lose all the money it had stood to gain by issuing new stock.

To address this type of situation, XYZ Company decides to issue subscription rights to its current shareholders. By issuing subscription rights, XYZ Company gives its investors "coupons" with which they can buy shares of the newly issued 200 shares for $8 per share rather than the $10 everyone else has to pay. These coupons, or subscription rights, are usually issued based on the number of shares already held by the current investor. In the same example, you own 100 shares, and XYZ Company has decided that for every 5 shares held by a current investor the investor will be issued one subscription right. You therefore have the right to purchase 20 shares for $8 each.

If you buy 20 additional shares at $8, it will cost you $160. That's a big break from the $200 it would cost a new investor to purchase those same 20 shares at $10 per share. And the value of your new shares is still $200, just as if you had paid the new-investor price of $10 per share. Thus you immediately make $40.

IMMEDIATE GRATIFICATION

The advantage of subscription rights is that you can make money from them even if you have no interest in purchasing additional stock. Let's say XYZ issues you 20 subscription rights and, truthfully, you have no intention of using them. Then let's say I'm an investor who wishes to purchase XYZ Company stock. You offer to sell me your 20 subscription rights for $1 each. Yes, you can do that because subscription rights are fully transferable; in other words, you can use them or dispose of them as you see fit.

I pay you $20 for your subscription rights and then buy the 20 shares at $8 each (20 × $8 = $160). Adding in the $20 I paid you initially, my total price is $180. I still got the stock $20 cheaper than if I had bought it in the open market at $10 per share. You've just made $20 from selling me something you didn't want anyway. As this example shows, subscription rights are really popular. They're like getting an unexpected gift. You are, however, still no longer half-owner in XYZ Company, but then it's not a perfect world.

WARRANTS

Warrants are very much like subscription rights in that they are usually used to purchase stock for less than what the stock is currently worth, or the *current market value*. Warrants differ from subscription rights in that subscription rights entitle the bearer to deduct a certain amount from the price of the stock, whereas warrants entitle the bearer to purchase the stock at a predetermined price, regardless of the current price the stock is selling for on the open market.

PLAIN ENGLISH

Warrants are a type of financial instrument distributed by the company that originally issued the corresponding stock. The warrants grant the bearer the right to purchase that company's stock at a predetermined price, regardless of the market value of the stock at that time.

For example, suppose that you have just purchased 10 shares of XYZ Company stock at $10 per share. XYZ Company knows that, as a new company, it may have a little difficulty finding new investors in the market right now, so the company attaches a warrant to each share that you have just purchased (free of charge, no less). The warrant entitles you to buy a share of XYZ Company stock for $11, regardless of what it's selling for on the market. Since you have just bought the stock for $10 per share, it would be kind of silly to pay $11 per share right now.

But, in the course of time, the price of XYZ Company rises to $13 per share. By cashing in your warrants, you could buy 10 more shares of XYZ Company stock at the price of $11 per share, thereby making an immediate profit of $20 ($11 × 10 = $110, versus $13 × 10 = $130).

Let's say that when you purchased those 10 initial shares and received the warrants, you were satisfied because you really only wanted 10 shares to begin with. You figured the warrants were nice but relatively useless, right? No. As in the subscription rights example, you can sell or otherwise dispose of warrants however you see fit. Therefore, if the price of XYZ Company stock rises to $13 per share, you have 10 warrants to use for purchasing that stock at $11 per share.

I'm an investor who wants to purchase XYZ Company stock, so you offer to sell me your warrants for $1 each. I use your warrants to purchase XYZ Company stock at $11 per share, and I still save $10 ($11 × 10 = 110 + $10 = $120, versus $13 × 10 = $130). You've just made $10 by selling me something you didn't want to begin with, and XYX Company has attracted a new investor. Everybody's happy.

MORE ON WARRANTS

Many investors buy and sell warrants, completely ignoring the underlying stock, because oftentimes more money can be made from the warrant transactions. For example, let's say you bought those 10 warrants from me at $1 each. Instead of using them to buy stock, you hold on to them and wait until the price of XYZ Company stock climbs to $14 per share. You then find another investor who is willing to pay $2 per warrant. The advantage to the buyer is that he or she acquires the right to buy XYZ Company shares at the bargain price of $11 each. The buyer will still save $10 in the transaction ($2 × 10 warrants = $20 and $11 × 10 shares = $110; $20 + $110 = $130, versus $140 to purchase 10 shares at $14). The investor has saved money, and you have made $10 from your initial $10 investment, effectively giving you a 100-percent profit.

Of course, if the price of XYZ Company stock never rises above $11 per share, you've just bought a dog with fleas. Welcome to the wonderful world of investing.

Also, it should be noted that XYZ Company is not issuing warrants for the sake of being nice. As noted in the previous example, companies typically issue stock because they are relatively young and/or may have a difficult time otherwise attracting new investors. Since warrants are almost always issued at a higher purchase price than what the stock is currently selling for, the company and the recipients of those warrants are all betting that the price of the stock will rise. Many times, those recipients are other companies or are brokerage houses, because companies often will pay each other off through the transfer of warrants. As in the example when no actual stock changed hands, these brokerage houses and companies will then sell the warrants to individual investors in order to raise cash without having to make a capital investment of their own, or with only a minimal one. In addition, this action effectively launches the warrants onto the common market for everyone to buy and sell.

OPTIONS

PLAIN ENGLISH

Options are a type of financial instrument granting the bearer the right to purchase or sell stock at a predetermined price. Options are not issued by the stock's company but are an agreement between two parties to buy or sell the stock between themselves.

Much like warrants, options entitle the bearer to buy or sell stock at a predetermined price within a certain time frame. An option that entitles the bearer to buy a stock is known as a *call*. An option that gives the bearer the right to sell the stock is a *put*. And the predetermined price at which the stock can be bought or sold is the *strike price*.

CALLS

By purchasing a *call option,* an investor is basically entering into a contract or agreement with the seller to purchase a stock at a predetermined price—the *strike price*. In gambling terms, you, the buyer, are betting that the price of the stock will go up; the seller of the option is betting that the price of the stock will stay the same or go down.

PLAIN ENGLISH

A **call** grants the bearer the option of purchasing stock at a predetermined price in the future, regardless of the stock's actual market value at that time.

It should be noted that the seller of the option doesn't necessarily have to own the stock for which he or she is selling the option. The seller of the option is responsible, however, for coming up with that stock for purchase at the strike price should the buyer of the option *exercise,* or use, the option. Should the stock be selling for a higher price on the open market, as is almost always the case, the seller would have to purchase the stock at the higher price and sell it for less than he or she paid for it.

LEVERAGE

On the other hand, an investor can often make (or lose) more money by purchasing options rather than by purchasing the actual stock. This is the concept known as *leverage.* The basic premise of leverage is the same as a see-saw: The further you get from the center, or fulcrum, the more dramatic the effects of movement. Leverage is explained in more detail in Lesson 9, "Opening a Brokerage Account," but let's see how the concept of leverage would work for an option.

Say you want to purchase 10 shares of XYZ Company stock, which is currently selling for $10 per share. However, you believe that the price of XYZ Company stock will rise to $15 per share. You could spend $100 to purchase the stock and wait. If the price should rise to $15, your stock would be worth $150. Thus, you would have made a $50 profit; not bad for a day's work. But let's say you decide instead to spend the money to buy 100 options at $1 per option. These options grant you the right to purchase the stock at $11. Now, should the price rise to $15 as in the first example, your options have an intrinsic value of $400. In other words, for each share of stock you bought at $11, you would automatically make a $4 profit off the $15 open market price. Since you have 100 options, you can make $400 profit immediately by exercising your option.

Or, even better, say you bought the 100 options for $1 and decided not to exercise them at all. Suppose you lacked the $1,100 needed to purchase those 100 shares at $11 in order to realize that $400 profit. You could always find another investor who wanted to purchase XYZ Company stock and offer to sell your options for $2 each (the dollar each you paid, plus a dollar in profit). You would make $100 and a 100 percent profit on the whole deal. The other investor would still save $200 on his or her purchase, and everyone would be happy. Well, unless you stuck with buying the stock instead of the options. Then you would make only $50 off the transaction.

On the downside, however, let's say that you spend that $100 to purchase those same options. And let's say that the other investor uses his or her $100 to purchase those 10 shares at $10 per share. And, let's say that the price of the stock drops to $9 and doesn't go up. Since the price of the stock never reaches the strike price of $11, your options are never exercisable; so you lose all of your $100. The other investor loses money also, but at least his or her stock is still worth $90. Or, even more insulting, should the price of XYZ Company stock stay the same, you've lost everything, whereas the other person who bought the stock hasn't gained, but hasn't lost a dime either. You're still out $100.

"Wait," you say, "Didn't you tell me in the last section that the price of stock will almost always go up eventually? So, I should just hold on to those options until such time as the stock does finally go up. Right?" Well, in theory the answer is yes. But to even the playing field, options have a limited time within which they must be exercised, or else they expire. The date when they expire is known as the *expiration date*. Although this term is not a particularly technical one, it is worth noting because it does limit the time within which an investor has a chance of making money off the option.

As noted earlier, an investor can often make more money with options than with an actual purchase of stock. However, the risks rise proportionately. The limited time frame and the increased effect from changes in the price of the stock are summed up in a term called *volatility*.

CAUTION

Volatility simply means that the more money you potentially can make with your investment, the more risk you run of losing your money. It is because of this increased volatility that options can be dangerous—even for seasoned investors.

For example, about three years ago I personally held several hundred options in a company, which were worth thousands of dollars. I kept meaning to convert the options to actual stock, but every time the stock rose a point, I made 10 times more profit than I would have had if I actually owned the stock itself. Those kinds of gains are really addictive, even to a seasoned investor like myself who knew the risks. At any rate, I never did convert the options. The day the Russian ruble collapsed, the underlying stock value dropped by half. This was disastrous for the stockholders because their stock lost half its value. However, I, as an option holder, was completely wiped out because the price of the stock had dropped below the strike price. My options were therefore completely worthless. Upset and in tears, not to mention broke, I called my parents to bemoan my disaster. That memory keeps me out of the options market, but you'll have to decide for yourself what your tolerance for risk is and act accordingly.

PUTS

Put options are the exact opposite of calls in that calls give the bearer the right to buy stock at a predetermined price, whereas puts give the bearer the right to *sell* his or her stock at a predetermined price. Please note that the bearer of a put has the right, but not the obligation, to sell those shares.

PLAIN ENGLISH

> A **put** grants the bearer the option of selling stock at a predetermined price in the future, regardless of the stock's actual market value at that time.

Let's assume that you already own 10 shares of XYZ Company stock for which you paid $10 per share. Then, let's assume that you are concerned that the price of your shares is about to drop. You might consider purchasing puts to hedge your losses. If you purchase 10 puts at $1 each to sell your stock at $9 per share, your total investment in XYZ Company stock and the puts would total $110 ($100 for the initial shares and $10 for the puts). Should the price of your stock drop to $7, you could exercise your options and sell the stock for $9 per share and recoup $90 of your money. Although you would still have suffered a $20 loss from your $110 investment, that is still better than the $30 loss you would have suffered by the declining price of your shares without the put option.

Again, even though the bearer is not obligated to sell the shares at any price, a substantial risk still applies. Let's say the price of XYZ Company stock never does drop, or even goes up. You would never exercise your options, since it would be silly to sell them for less than you could get on the open market. Like a call, a put also has a time limit within which it must be exercised, or else it expires. Should you reach the expiration date without exercising your options, you would lose the entire $10 you paid for the options.

OWNERSHIP NOT REQUIRED

Like the call, you don't actually have to own the underlying stock in order to make money from a put option. Let's say for example, that XYZ Company stock is selling for $10 per share. You believe that the price of XYZ Company will drop. It certainly doesn't make sense to purchase stock in a company with shares you believe will drop in value. Through the use of a put, however, you can still make a profit from this situation.

Since you believe the price of XYZ Company stock will drop, you consider purchasing 10 put options at $1 per option. This would cost you $10. Then the price does in fact drop to $6 per share. But you didn't actually purchase any shares of XYZ stock, so you have no stock with which to exercise the option. No matter; you find another investor who does own 10 shares of XYZ Company stock and is looking to get rid of them. You sell him or her your options for $2 each—the dollar you paid and a dollar profit on each put. You have just made $10 from your initial $10 investment, so you are ahead 100 percent. The buyer of your options sells his or her shares at $9 each for a total of $90; after subtracting the $20 paid to you for the options, the buyer's total is $70. Not a great day by any means but still $10 better than having sold the shares at $6 per share for a total of $60.

On the other side, if you were the seller of the options, you could make a quick and easy $10 from selling the put. For the record, the put price of an option is also known as its *premium*. Should the price of XYZ Company stock never go up, or at least stay the same, the put owner would never exercise his or her option; and upon the expiration date, you would be $10 richer for doing absolutely nothing more than making a promise on which you never had to make good.

Before you get too excited and start selling puts, be aware that you would be responsible for purchasing the stock from the put holder on demand, regardless of what the price on the open market is. Whether or not you own stock in this case is irrelevant, because if the price of XYZ Company stock drops to $1 per share you are still required to purchase the put holder's shares for $10 per share. Some of this $9 per share loss would be offset by the money you make from selling the put, but you would nevertheless have lost significant amounts.

It is imperative therefore to always read the fine print and know what you are getting into, especially with anything as volatile as options.

STOCK INDEX OPTIONS

Stock index options work the same as regular options except that instead of being pegged to the market price of an underlying stock, they are pegged to the price of the entire market. Huh? We will get into stock indexes in detail in Lesson 15, "The Ticker Tape, Stock Indices, and Other Media," but for our present purposes let's use this next example.

Stocks and derivatives are bought and sold like anything else in markets. Let's use your local farmer's market as an example. You are not the guy selling tomatoes at the market, but rather the guy who owns the land on which the market sits. You make your money renting booths to sellers at the farmer's market. You notice that these days the tomato seller is making more money selling tomatoes than she used to, and you're wondering if you should be charging more for booth spaces. How do you figure out whether the entire market is making more money than it used to?

You could add up the individual sale prices of all the items (tomatoes, corn, flowers, etc.) at last year's market and then divide the total by the number of items on the list. This would give you a very rough average price of the items for sale. If a year later you added up the current prices of those same items and divided the total by the same number, you would probably get a different average. If the new average were higher, it's a pretty safe bet all the sellers at the market were making a little more than they used to and you should raise your booth rent proportionately. If the new average were lower or stayed the same, you should probably consider leaving your prices as they are, or even reducing them.

PLAIN ENGLISH

Stock index options are options to buy or sell stock whose price represents the value of the entire market at a predetermined price, regardless of the actual value of the market.

Stock indexes work on the same principle as the farmer's market example. They also facilitate trading for those investors whose trades are based on the markets rather than individual stocks. Let's say, for example, that you believe the stock index will rise $1 a day for the next two weeks. Because the index is an average, some of the listed stocks will gain value and some will lose value, but you believe that overall the market average will rise. You could buy one share of every stock on the index if you were so inclined. Be warned that indexes are usually composed of hundreds and even thousands of stocks, so this idea is pretty impractical. The bookkeeping alone would be a nightmare, and you would need zillions of dollars to buy at least one share of everything on the index as well as pay all the service charges. Instead, you could buy a stock index put and wait for the index to go up. Since you believe the stock index will go down, you would buy a stock index call to achieve the same result.

American Depository Receipts (ADRs)

American Depository Receipts (ADRs) are one of my favorites, because they work the exact opposite of most derivatives. Instead of making things more complicated, ADRs simplify things for the average investor. *ADRs* are stocks in pools that comprise foreign stocks.

For example, let's say you've heard of this great company in Mexico, Widgeto Incorporado. You really want to invest in that company, as you've just read they've invented a new widget made out of adobe. You're convinced the value of Widgeto Incorporado stock is about to go through the roof.

You could open up a brokerage account in Mexico and go through the normal procedures to buy Widgeto Incorporado. But, in all honesty, the paperwork involved would be horrendous. Being a foreign investor in Mexico would be a problem, and such issues as exchange rates and taxation would be problematic when you tried to bring your profits back to the United States. The kinds of problems encountered in this type of transaction scare away almost all individual investors, leaving this type of investment pretty much the stomping ground of brokerage houses, banks, and other entities large enough to maintain staffs to deal with all the headaches.

Luckily, these brokerage houses and banks want to do business with you. They've heard the concerns of you and many of their other investors about not being able to invest in foreign markets. To address this situation, they have come up with the concept of ADRs. A brokerage house or bank goes to Mexico and buys a big pool of Widgeto Incorporado stock and then places the shares *in trust*.

PLAIN ENGLISH

In trust means committing or giving custody of something (in this case, stock) to an entity (a bank, for example) to be safekept and administered for the benefit of someone else (investors).

The institution then issues shares in the pool of Widgeto Incorporado stock. These shares, or ADRs, are American shares and trade as such, even though they ultimately end up representing ownership in a foreign stock. The price of the ADR will reflect the price of the foreign stock; as it goes up or down, so will the corresponding ADRs. With little or no effort, American investors are free to invest in foreign markets.

Like any investment vehicle, ADRs have some drawbacks. Be aware that an ADR represents ownership in a foreign stock—it's not actually ownership of that stock but rather of the trust pool. This arrangement has minimal drawbacks, but, all things being equal, real ownership is usually a little more secure. A more pressing issue is exchange rate. The stock pool will be affected by any movements in the exchange rates between pesos and dollars, which could diminish any profits American investors might be able to make from the foreign investment. A quick review of the exchange rate is therefore probably a good idea before purchasing an ADR.

THE 30-SECOND RECAP

- A subscription right enables current shareholders to purchase additional shares of a company's future-issued stock at a discount from the market price at that time.

- Warrants are a "coupon" with which the bearer can purchase additional shares of a company's stock at a set price. Warrants are issued by the stock's issuing company.

- Calls represent an agreement between two parties whereby the bearer purchases from the seller the right to purchase stock at a later date from him or her at a predetermined price; in theory, below the market price of the stock at that time.

- Puts represent an agreement between two parties whereby the bearer purchases from the seller the right to later sell stock to him or her at a predetermined price; in theory, above the market price of the stock at that time.

- Stock index options represent a call or a put whose price is not based on an individual stock, but rather on the value of the entire market as based on a market indicator or index.

- ADRs are international stocks held in trust or custodial pools by a domestic entity for the purpose of accessibility to domestic investors. The purchase of an ADR does not provide ownership of the actual underlying stock, but of the trust or custodial pool.

LESSON 7
The Markets

In this lesson you will learn about the physical locations where stock is available for trade and also about computerized networks over which stock is available for trade.

TRADING PLACES

So, where are all these trades taking place? Way before there was money, people used to trade items to each other. If I had a goat and you wanted it, you'd offer me three chickens in trade, and we'd both go off happy. If someone else offered me four chickens, or if someone else showed up with a bigger goat, there would probably be a lot of yelling involved. Eventually, people finally figured out that they'd save time looking for other people with whom to trade if they regularly showed up at one designated location where everyone brought something to trade.

With the introduction of money, these trades evolved into purchases and sales. Thousands of years later, the market concept is still very much alive. People who want to buy or sell stocks figure that showing up at the same location at the same time to trade stocks is a pretty good idea. Today, over 140 physical exchanges buy and sell trillions of shares of hundreds of thousands of stocks 24 hours per day. Although those figures are mind-boggling, they represent only a small fraction of the trades being conducted over computerized networks.

Here are the markets:

- **New York Stock Exchange (NYSE).** The largest physical stock exchange in the world.

- **American Stock Exchange (AMEX).** The rival of the NYSE in size and prestige.

- **Regional exchanges.** Fourteen exchanges located around the United States.

- **Over the counter.** A term for stocks traded over a computerized network called the National Market System (NMS).

- **International exchanges.** Stock exchanges in other countries.

- **Other markets.** Markets where the trading of financial instruments other than stocks, such as futures, options, and money, is conducted.

THE NEW YORK STOCK EXCHANGE

Back in 1792, 24 men showed up to trade stocks under a buttonwood tree and pronounced that location as their future stock-trading marketplace. The road next to the buttonwood tree had been named for a blockade wall built earlier to keep Manhattan settlers safe from marauding Indians and pirates. I'm not making this up. That market and its humble beginnings eventually evolved into today's mammoth New York Stock Exchange, and the corresponding road next to the blockade wall became known as Wall Street, synonymous with today's financial world.

PLAIN ENGLISH

The **markets** is a term referring to the centralized physical locations and the computer networks at which the business of trading stocks is conducted.

The New York Stock Exchange (NYSE) is, hands down, the world's most famous and powerful exchange as well as the largest stock exchange in the world. The ramifications of a day's trades at this exchange are worldwide and affect commerce and governments alike. For all its bedlam though, the NYSE trades only about 1,600 of the country's biggest stocks. "Biggest" meaning no company with less than $18 million in assets or less than 1.1 million issued shares need apply for a listing. Although the stock you purchase may be listed on the exchange, this is definitely not the arena for individual investors. It is, however, a super-cool place to visit if you are ever in New York. The exchange offers tours that prove the movies are neither lying nor exaggerating when they portray the exchange as a bedlam of screaming and waving.

THE AMERICAN STOCK EXCHANGE

The *American Stock Exchange (AMEX)* is also based in New York and has a great tale of origin. In 1842 men who were not considered "gentlemanly enough" to be admitted into the New York Stock Exchange stood outside the building, trading stocks on the curb and yelling and hollering loud enough to ensure that they were being heard by the "gentlemen" inside. These rabble-rousers, known as the New York Curb Exchange, traded stocks in this manner until 1921 when they finally moved indoors. Subsequently, in 1953 this exchange changed its name to The American Stock Exchange.

PLAIN ENGLISH

The **American Stock Exchange** is the New York Stock Exchange's rival trading 900 of the nation's largest stock to the NYSE's 1,600. In addition, the AMEX requires the issuing company to maintain a balance of $4 million in assets to the NYSE's minimum requirement of $18 million.

AMEX's beginnings as a rogue market make for a good story, but the truth today is somewhat less wayward. To this day, AMEX is still NYSE's closest competitor both in size and in scope, trading about 900 of the country's biggest stocks. To be listed on the AMEX, a company must maintain a minimum of $4 million dollars in assets and have issued a minimum of a half million shares of stock. For the same reasons as at the NYSE, few if any individuals conduct their trading business here.

REGIONAL EXCHANGES

The two principal markets in the United States, the NYSE and AMEX, can actively trade only a minuscule proportion of the total number of shares in the United States. For that reason, 14 other smaller exchanges, which are scattered around the country, are linked to the NYSE and the AMEX in order to help them trade stock more quickly and effectively. These exchanges, known as *regional exchanges,* operate the same as the two big exchanges, and often even duplicate their work.

Some of the better-known regional exchanges are ...

- Pacific Stock Exchange

- Boston Stock Exchange

- Midwest Stock Exchange

- Philadelphia Stock Exchange

These exchanges, while perhaps not quite as well known as NYSE and AMEX, are significant in their own right for many reasons. The Philadelphia Stock Exchange, for example, has the distinction of being this country's first stock exchange. Its founding in 1790 predates the founding of the NYSE by more than a quarter of a century, and the founding of AMEX by over half a century.

Again, many of these exchanges trade the same stocks as their bigger counterparts to help reduce the load that the major exchanges are expected to service. At the end of the day, the results of trading a particular stock are added up from all locations and reported to the general public as *composite trading.*

Think of the situation as a burger joint. The entire country couldn't walk into the same burger joint and expect to be served within a reasonable time frame. So, the burger joint opens up locations all over the country, and they all offer the same food to their customers. In the same way, the regional exchanges offer the same stocks for trade to local investors as the big ones do. At the end of the day, however, management wants to know how many burgers were sold at all locations. After adding together the sales at all locations, the resulting total number of burgers sold is known as the burger joint's composite trading figure.

SMALL FRY REGIONAL EXCHANGES

Regional exchanges conduct their own proprietary business as well business for their bigger counterparts. The requirements for a company to have its stock listed on the two major exchanges are often prohibitive for many smaller companies. However, these companies can usually meet the requirements of the smaller exchanges and for that reason are traded there.

For example, in the same burger joint scenario let's say you are a lobster fisherman. You know that the national burger joint has no interest in your new product, the Lobster Burger. In Maine, however, the Lobster Burger is a big hit. Rather than attempting to sell your Lobster Burger to Burger Joint headquarters for distribution in all its locations, you take your Lobster Burger idea directly to Burger Joint headquarters for the State of Maine. They agree to distribute, or sell, your Lobster Burger exclusively through Maine. In the same way, a regional exchange offers access to markets where many smaller companies can remain competitive.

OVER THE COUNTER

The least prestigious and most obscure market to the public is also without a doubt the single largest. The vast majority of stocks don't trade in the previously described physical markets at all. Rather, they trade on a highly sophisticated computer network called the National Market System (NMS). The NMS is absolutely massive in scope, listing and trading trillions of shares of thousands upon thousands of different stocks.

The number of trades and stock listed on the *over the counter (OTC)* market dwarfs any physical exchange anywhere. However, as OTC is a computerized network rather than a physical marketplace, it does not maintain the glamour of old buildings and yelling traders. For that reason, many people will erroneously omit the OTC when discussing markets.

PLAIN ENGLISH

Over the counter (OTC) is a term for stocks that are traded over a computerized network known as the NMS, the largest stock-trading network in the world.

In addition, the number of traders using NMS dwarfs the number of physical traders. While the crowds on the floors of the physical exchanges sometimes barely fit in the building, they represent only a small percentage of a fraction of the number of traders with access to NMS. NMS traders sit in offices all over the country, accessing NMS through computer terminals and conducting trades over the telephone.

"Wait a second," you wonder, "how could a trading network that large go undetected to the general public?" Well, in truth it hasn't. The members of the NMS network are governed by an association known as the National Association of Securities Dealers (NASD). The results of the day's trading over the NMS are reported to the general public as the National Association of Securities Dealers Automated Quotations, or NASDAQ. Ever seen that one in the newspapers?

Since NMS is so large in scope, attempting to report the entirety of even a single day's trading would create a document the size of the New York City phone book. NASDAQ therefore breaks down its listings by relevance, so investors (or anyone else) can search subdivided listings to learn the fate of their stock's performance. *The Wall Street Journal,* for example, includes these subdivisions:

- **National Market Issues.** This listing reports on the activity of the most actively traded over-the-counter stocks. As a result, the information is usually the most widely reported and comprehensive in scope.

- **NASDAQ Bid and Asked Quotations.** This listing usually covers the second most actively traded set of stocks. The information reported daily is less comprehensive in scope than National Market Issues and is a little less widely reported.

- **Additional OTC Quotes.** Even though these are the least active of all the reported over-the-counter trades, they are still active enough to merit widespread reporting. Reported information is limited to the highest bid price of a stock and the lowest asking price of the stock for a single day's trading.

INTERNATIONAL EXCHANGES

The scope of American finance is absolutely unparalleled anywhere else on the globe. The American economy is somewhere around 16 times the size of its closest competitor. The sixth largest economy on the face of the earth, for example, is that of the State of California. For all its size, however, the U.S. economy does not, by any stretch of the imagination, stand alone. Exchanges and financial markets all over the world, through the use of today's computerized systems, have created a world where stocks trade 24 hours per day.

Exchanges exist in almost every major city in the world, including Paris, London, Frankfurt, Tokyo, Johannesburg, Sidney, Hong Kong, and Singapore. While every one of these exchanges directly affects, and is directly affected by, each other, they are all under the authority of their own governments and must follow their government's laws. As a result, they differ from each as much as they are the same. While learning about international markets is interesting, actually investing in them as an individual is an altogether different matter. As a general rule, most international investing is done by corporate entities such as banks or mutual funds which then provide opportunities for international investments domestically through the use of ADRs or globally invested funds.

> **CAUTION**
> Moving money and stock from country to country is a very difficult transaction as a result of conflicting tax structures, exchange rates, and permissible investments.

In addition, although the activities of the international exchanges are not as widely reported in the United States as those of our own exchanges, that fact in no way reflects badly on the prestige or importance of these markets. Several of these exchanges, for example, predate the founding of either or both of the major American exchanges. London claims the world's oldest stock exchange, having been founded in 1773.

The results of the day's trading in international exchanges are readily available in the United States, though the reports are not as extensive as for the U.S. exchanges. Many financial publications list the results of any day's trades in a number of financial markets. *The Wall Street Journal* and *The New York Times* both publish the results of the most actively traded stocks worldwide. Your local paper may track some foreign holdings, too. (This will be discussed in greater detail in Lesson 14, "How to Check Your Investments.")

THE BIG BANG

Even if you don't actually own stock in foreign companies, their performance can provide great insight into the future performance of the American markets. The day of the *Big Bang* marked the beginning of a global market. As the increased globalization of trades continues, the effects of a day's trading around the world will continue to directly affect the performance of other international markets. A recent example was the collapse of many Asian markets, an event that dealt a fierce blow to the stability of the American markets. International investors who were awake during the open hours of Asian trading were aware of the impending damage hours before the American exchanges even opened. In this particular example, I'm proud to say that the American markets were strong enough to withstand the blow, and the damage was quickly repaired.

PLAIN ENGLISH

The **Big Bang** was a red-letter day in trading history. On October 27, 1986, the London Stock Exchange dropped its restrictions on allowing foreign investors to participate in their markets. Symbolically, this day represents the unification of markets around the world into one global marketplace.

OTHER MARKETS

In addition to the markets already discussed, which deal primarily with stock, a number of different markets exist to service the trades of derivatives, options, futures, and other stock-like investments. These niche exchanges are of great importance to their particular products, although their exchanges may not be as widely known.

The Chicago Board of Trade, for example, deals almost exclusively with the exchange of grain futures. The New York Cotton Exchange deals with cotton, of course. These specialty markets rarely make for exciting financial news, yet the Chicago Board of Trade, for example, is one of the most important exchanges in the world. A day's activity here could determine changes in the *consumer price index,* an indicator that measures the percentage of change of the cost of goods and services in well-developed nations and that also measures the end or beginning of famine in emerging markets.

PLAIN ENGLISH

> Remember that stock index explanation from Lesson 6, whereby an average would indicate whether the price of everything in the market had gone up? The **consumer price index** is the same thing, except that instead of averaging the cost of stock or a farmer's market, it averages the cost of all things the average person in this country buys, like food, clothing, and utilities.

Most of these exchanges operate on basically the same principle as the stock exchanges, but their clientele as well as their purpose are usually substantially more specific. In addition, the governing entities may be different from their stock exchange counterparts. The exchange of futures, for example, is regulated by the Commodity Futures Trading Commission (CFTC) rather than by the Securities and Exchange Commission (SEC). Like stock exchanges, these various exchanges are located around the country, in Chicago, Minneapolis, and Philadelphia, as well as around the world, in Paris, Winnipeg, and Sydney.

Finally, be aware that in the past the activity of these various exchanges could be a little more difficult to find. Usually only the very large financial publications such as *The Wall Street Journal* or corresponding local publications carried the reports. Fortunately, today's computers and dedicated financial media are so broad that information on any of these markets is usually available at the touch of a button.

THE 30-SECOND RECAP

- The most powerful, prestigious, and largest physical exchange in the world is the NYSE.

- The AMEX is a massive physical exchange rived by only the NYSE in power, prestige, and size.

- Fourteen smaller regional exchanges that trade the stock of NYSE and AMEX as well as their own proprietary issues are located strategically around the United States.

- Over the counter refers to stocks traded over a computerized network known as the National Market System. These trades compose the largest market in the world.

- International exchanges are any physical exchanges located around the world, ranging from London to Johannesburg to Tokyo.

- Other markets refers to specialized markets and exchanges for niche products such as grains, futures, and options.

LESSON 8

Brokers and Brokerage Houses

In this lesson you will learn about the various types of stockbrokers and about brokerage houses where you can purchase stock.

TYPES OF STOCKBROKERS

Stocks are available for sale through stockbrokers. You can find many listings for brokers in Appendix B, "Resources," at the end of this book, in the financial pages of your local newspaper, or even in your local Yellow Pages. You will find

- Full service brokers

- Discount brokers

- E-brokers

ROLE OF STOCKBROKERS

The term *broker* has been used to describe financial transaction agents since the seventeenth century. Brokers are part of a bigger category known as investment bankers, a group that is also not new. Investment bankers have been around since at least the Middle Ages when they were responsible for raising the monies necessary for kings and queens to wage war on one another. The adjective "investment" describing banker only means that the banker focuses on investment as opposed to other banker functions such as retail banking, which deals with such things as checking and savings for the general public.

Modern standards are substantially less dramatic and violent. A stockbroker today is a person who has passed a test called a Series 7 Exam administered by the Securities and Exchange Commission (SEC) and, as such, has the necessary qualifications to buy and sell stock for his or her clients. A brokerage firm is nothing more than a firm composed of, you guessed it, stockbrokers.

What kind of people become stockbrokers? Those who obviously have some sort of interest in finance, economics, and the stock market. This would be necessary, as the Series 7 exam is not easy and the career of a stockbroker, because of the high pressure, is generally pretty short (about two to three years). For those reasons, most brokerage houses will pay for new brokers to take classes, similar to preparing for the SAT, and even pay for the new broker to take the exam. The new broker would then, however, be committed to work for the brokerage house for a period of time, again, usually a couple of years. Most of the people who go through this are also attracted by the availability of high income. As brokers work on commission, their pay is directly tied to how motivated they are to sell stock. An aggressive broker can make hundreds of thousands, or even millions of dollars per year.

In addition to having the qualifications including licensing and knowledge of stocks and the markets, brokers are the only ones legally permitted to buy and sell stock, so they've got a lock on the market. Like it or not, you've got to use a broker or brokerage firm to buy stocks.

Luckily, since the abolishment of standardized broker fees in 1975, many different types and price structures for stockbrokers now exist. Everyone has access to any number of competing firms, so you can pick the type of broker or brokerage that is most applicable to your needs.

SECURITIES AND EXCHANGE COMMISSION

The *Securities and Exchange Commission (SEC)* is the U.S. Government commission charged with the responsibility of ensuring compliance with its securities act. Through the use of its own financial professionals, which includes qualified stockbrokers, the SEC monitors trading and the markets through the computerized networks for strange and/or unusual trading activity, for example. These professionals would then further investigate to uncover illegal activity such as insider trading (trading with prior or nonpublic information). To eliminate conflict of interests, SEC financial professionals do not engage in professional trading activity themselves, but work for and are compensated exclusively by the U.S. Government.

PLAIN ENGLISH

The **Securities and Exchange Commission (SEC)** acts as the stock market police. The SEC makes sure everyone is following the stock laws, or securities acts, passed by the U.S. Government.

FULL SERVICE STOCKBROKERS

You can find full service stockbrokers at the most well-known and established companies, including

- Salomon Smith Barney

- Morgan Stanley

- Goldman Sachs

- Merrill Lynch

For all their eminent reputations, however, brokerage firms use a substantially different track for selling stock than the average investor would think. The company that uses the expression about making money the old-fashioned way—earning it—isn't lying. They just didn't specify for *whom* they were making that old-fashioned money.

Bluntly put, stockbrokers have to make a living, too. And that lifestyle isn't cheap. Did I mention that full service brokers also charge the highest commissions? I've heard of full service brokers who charge up to $75 *per transaction*. Even though the average investor may be aware of these commissions, what goes largely unsaid is the other ways in which stockbrokers make money or further their business.

You should know upfront that in all fairness, full service brokers and brokerages have their uses and place within investment. Many people, for a variety of reasons, do utilize the services of full service brokers and brokerages and do very well by them.

For example, someone with enough money in the market to prohibit the time needed to effectively keep track of investment trends (because the person is using all that time to make the money that's being invested) would make a good candidate for a full service broker.

Also, someone who was planning to buy and/or sell on a daily basis is an example of someone who might fare well using the services of a broker. Although this type of client, however, would still do well to consider excessive service fees involved in these kinds of services. In addition, most stockbrokers aren't dishonest and do play upfront with their clients. After all, unhappy clients will leave sooner or later, so it's in the stockbroker's best interest to keep them happy.

The average stockbroker, however, does have to make a living. So, for example, a stockbroker with his or her huge wealth of knowledge tells you that purchasing stock in XYZ Company is the single best thing you can do. You invest as the stockbroker tells you to; after all, who are you to second-guess the stockbroker? You're a dentist with little or no knowledge of how all this works, whereas the broker has years of experience and access to a substantial amount of firm research— usually from within the brokerage house itself. So, the stockbroker takes a commission for placing the purchase order. The stockbroker is happy; you're happy. What could be wrong?

Did the stockbroker mention that the reason you should buy XYZ Company stock is also because he or she needs to sell a certain amount of XYZ Company's stock in order to retain his or her account, and the broker was running pretty close to the end of the month without having reached that quota? Or did the stockbroker mention that the company is giving him or her a cut of the sale out of the backside for each share the broker places with a client? The stockbroker wasn't lying about XYZ Company stock being the best purchase you could make. The broker just failed to mention that the payday was his or hers, not yours.

Also, the "research" that you thought would make a difference, and that went largely unnoticed in this transaction was flawed anyway. The analysts who compile this research are under extraordinary pressure from upper management as well as from the clients themselves to back up the interests of the company. Not necessarily to lie, mind you, but to present the information in its best—or in the case of the competitor, the worst—possible light.

CAUTION

A full service broker usually manages his or her client's account directly and charges the highest commissions.

And finally, from personal experience, many people develop a good working relationship with their brokers and a strong sense of loyalty keeps them as clients. Even in these situations, however, be aware of the whole story.

THE LOYAL LOSER

For example, I personally fall into that last category. A couple of years ago I hired a full service broker from a well-known firm for some of my accounts. She was a nice young person, and I liked her so much that I was loath to leave her *even though I consistently lost money with her management*. I took the losses without saying a word, because I figured we were friends. So did she—until she got a promotion and turned over all her portfolios to a replacement. The new broker was even nicer and friendlier than the first, but she was a goner before she unpacked her nametag. I closed my account immediately.

The point here is that I was looking to make a profit, not new friends. The first broker, really, was a nice person, and probably used a lot of that friendliness to keep clients such as me. She certainly wasn't keeping clients because of the profits we were making.

As for the second broker, I never lost a cent, but that was because I finally wised up to the fact that I was keeping these professionals on my payroll because they were friendly, not effective. Who would keep a plumber on staff when all the faucets still leak? In all fairness, the replacement broker may have been poised to make me a great deal of profit, but I had decided by that point to take control of my money and manage it myself.

CUTTING YOUR LOSSES

I lost a friend, but I'm not losing money anymore. I should also point out that the investments I made on my own during that time made excellent gains. And what's most relevant about that example isn't so much the broker story as it is the fact that I made more money by managing my own investments. Had I lost more money through my own transactions, that would have been okay, too. At least I would have been responsible either way since I was making my own decisions regarding my money.

The point is this—control your own money in all aspects. This means that even if you do hire a professional to help you, you are still responsible for ensuring that the person you choose is effectively doing exactly what you hired him or her to accomplish. Make sure then, that you periodically reevaluate their performance. Don't get sidetracked by things like emotion or friendship. As with any professionals, if they are not cutting the mustard, get rid of them and hire someone better.

DISCOUNT STOCKBROKERS

In 1975, standardized brokerage prices were abolished by the government. Prior to that time, buying a share of stock cost the same

regardless of where it was purchased. The change in the law meant
that brokers and brokerages were left to their own devices to determine how much their services were worth, and investors were finally
free to decide how much they were willing to pay. That, coupled with
the proliferation of information via the media and Internet along with
the explosive growth of individual investors (we do talk amongst our-
selves after all), led to the introduction of a whole new breed of brokerage, the discount brokerage.

Discount brokers all have one thing in common: You pay for what you
get. In the world of full service brokers, investors are usually charged
the same price regardless of how many of the brokerage's services
they utilize. Most discount brokerages have a price structure broken
down like a menu. If you want advice, it costs a dollar. You want to
place your trade in person? That costs another dollar. The benefit to
this, of course, is that if you already know which stock you want to
buy, you will pay much less to simply place the purchase order than
the investor who wants to sit with the broker for three hours discussing his or her options.

PLAIN ENGLISH

> A **discount broker** provides his or her services piece-
> meal or à la carte. Discount broker clients are usually
> charged only for the services they use.

In addition, discount brokerages are no longer the renegade firms of
Wall Street. The full service brokerages learned quickly that in the
evolving world of finance they either adapted their price structure or
died. That being the case, almost all of the full service brokerages
introduced discount brokerage services within their own firm or in a
subsidiary. Investors are now free to have their cake and eat it, too:
With this setup, when you need full service, you get it (and you pay
for it, too); and when you simply need an action (such as buying or
selling a share of stock), you get that, too.

You can find discount brokers advertised in any of the places you find full service brokers—Appendix B, the financial pages of your local newspaper, and so on. When contacting the brokerage firms, most will tell you up front what services and plans they offer (much like checking and savings accounts at your local bank) and you would then choose those services or plans that most appeal to you.

E-BROKERS

The growth of the Internet threw a new star into the ring: the *e-brokerage*. These include companies like Ameritech, LBJ Direct, and E-Trade. Many of these electronic brokerages have grown to massive sizes in their few years of existence, verifying their popularity. The e-brokerages have many things going for them, not the least of which is their prices.

PLAIN ENGLISH

> **E-brokers** are completely licensed to provide all the services of a traditional brokerage online. E-brokerages accept trades 24 per day, 7 days per week, Be aware, however, that the order is usually retained until the physical markets open.

Because e-brokerages are virtual firms, they have little or no overhead. They have no need for expensive items such as prestigious office buildings. Since they send their quarterly statements via e-mail, they save money on paper and printing costs. With orders being sent in electronically, staff costs are minimal. As a result, the cost for a basic purchase or sale of stock can be as low as $7. That's almost a tenth of the $75 cost of the full service broker price mentioned earlier. Warning bells are going off in your head. "There must be a catch," you say. Depending on what kind of investor you want to become, there might be. However, most of the loopholes have already been addressed directly.

For example, investors who want information on stocks, trends, market happenings, etc., will find it supplied in the electronic library of the e-brokerage. Unlike full service and discount brokerages, they provide it free of cost. Daily stock and market updates are also available online, as are advice and answers to specific questions from investors. Again, all of these services are available online, and they're free. The investor is, of course, charged with the responsibility of doing the footwork, researching the stock and reading up on market trends—something many, many investors simply don't like doing.

Should you have a problem or dislike typing in the order and want to speak to a live person, that service is also available. However, be aware that there is usually an extra charge for that service, and you run the risk of looking very 1980s.

E-brokerages have come along last in the line of brokerage services. Thus they have had ample opportunity to see what the average investor wanted in a brokerage and adapted brilliantly to fill those needs. The biggest disadvantage of the e-broker is also its greatest appeal. The investor is directly responsible for the decisions concerning his or her own money and investments.

EDUCATE YOURSELF

The irony of the brokers and brokerage houses is that they create the need for an investor to educate him- or herself further regarding money management. This is a good thing. Depending on what type of brokerage service you select, minimum or maximum, you as the investor are ultimately responsible for ensuring your money is being effectively managed and you are being appropriately charged. Whether that means researching the trade yourself or researching the returns from your professional's advice, you make the call. This is your hard-earned cash—make sure you know where every dime of it is going.

THE 30-SECOND RECAP

- Full service brokers have passed the Series 7 exam and are therefore licensed to provide all investment services. Full service brokers are usually very hands on, managing their clients' accounts directly, and charge the highest fees.

- Discount brokers provide investment services piecemeal or à la carte, as preferred by the client. Discount broker clients are usually charged only for the services they use, generally less than full service brokers.

- E-brokers provide all investment services online. Additional services are also usually available on the telephone or through a live broker, although additional fees usually apply. E-brokers generally charge the least of the various brokers.

Lesson 9

Opening a Brokerage Account

In this lesson you will learn about the various types of brokerage accounts that are available and the differences in how they operate.

Getting Started

Opening a brokerage account is a relatively simple procedure. On average, most brokerage firms will open an account for about $2,500. However, as this is an average, the initial amount may vary. Many brokerages offer accounts at various levels with a number of enticements to make the investor open the account with as much money as possible. Open an account at $10,000 and you get a toaster. Open an account with $100,000 and someone from the brokerage will come to your house to make the toast. See how that works?

In all seriousness, the fight for new investors is fierce and you can make out as the various brokers battle for your business. Most e-brokers are currently offering everything from reduced trade prices to outright free trades for an extended period of time, a year for example, if you commit to keeping your account with them. Whether you open an account online, by telephone, or in person, be sure and ask what kind of perks are available or you might miss out on a great deal.

In addition, regardless of what type of broker you will be using, it's probably a pretty good idea to get information on a couple of different ones before making your decision. Any legitimate broker will be happy to give you almost any type of information or reference you wish to see.

Not all brokerages require such large initial deposits when opening new accounts. To most people, $2,500 is an astronomical sum, and that's not so strange. The average person simply doesn't have $2,500 lying around the house not being otherwise used. A number of brokerages do allow smaller initial investment amounts of $1,000 or even $500. In addition, many brokerages will allow you to open an account with a small amount if you agree to *systematic deposits.* This is a great way to build up a brokerage account by opening the account with a minimum amount, often as low as $50 or $100, and investing that same amount each month. All you need to do is forward your bank account number and a signed authorization and that set amount will be automatically deducted on the same day each month.

PLAIN ENGLISH

A **systematic deposit** is a predetermined amount that is regularly deposited to an account. For example, every month on payday you send $50 to your account. This service is offered by almost any broker.

Finally, many brokerage houses run sales. I'm not making this up. The competition for investors has become so fierce in the last couple of years that brokerage houses will allow clients to open accounts with amounts substantially below their normal minimum limits. After all, it's in the brokerage's best interests to hold $200 of an investor's money rather than nothing at all.

FILL OUT THIS FORM, PLEASE

Once the amount has been established, you as a new investor simply fill out a new account form just as you would at any bank. Although the information required varies, certain information remains standard. The following list is not meant to be exhaustive, but you should probably be prepared to supply some or all of the following information:

Your name

Your address

Your Social Security Number

The name of your bank and your account numbers there

Account numbers at different brokerages (if applicable)

Your employer

Annual income

Net worth

Your investment objectives

Citizenship

Age

In addition, when opening a joint account, your spouse will probably be required to provide all or some of this information as well. Finally, a credit check may be run on you. Bad credit will not necessarily prevent you from opening an account; after all, the brokerage houses don't grow by passing up new business. However, nor do they grow by making bad decisions regarding deadbeat clients, so it's a good idea to check your credit rating and straighten out any discrepancies beforehand.

TIP

> Getting a copy of your credit report is a good idea before beginning any financial activity. Appendix B, "Resources," contains contact information on the two largest credit reporting agencies in the United States. A copy of your credit report is available free upon request from each.

Once you are fully ready to open your account, which type will you choose? The two most popular brokerage accounts are …

- Cash account

- Margin account

CASH ACCOUNT

A *cash account* is the more popular. It's certainly the safest one to keep you, as a new investor, out of trouble while learning your way through the stock market. In simplest terms, a cash account enables you to buy and sell stock in direct proportion to what is in your account. This means that if you have $1,000 in your account, you can buy only $993 worth of stock in XYZ Company. Wait, what happened to the other $7? It went to pay the brokerage for placing the purchase, remember?

> ### PLAIN ENGLISH
>
> A **cash account** is a brokerage account in which the investor can purchase stock only in an amount equivalent to the amount of money being maintained within the account.

It is exactly this type of example that shows the advantage of a cash account, and new investors should strongly consider having one. With a cash account, if you had tried to place an order for $1,000 worth of stock, the brokerage would have informed you that you didn't have sufficient money in your account, or they simply wouldn't have placed the order.

In the worst-case scenario, the brokerage would simply either freeze your account until such time as you coughed up the $7, cancel the purchase, or otherwise deal with the situation. Many brokerages will still allow you to make trades, as long as you put up the cash, and will freeze only the amount in question. In any event, you would definitely be aware of what was going on or what had already happened, and nothing would have happened that could get you into financial trouble.

SAFEGUARDING YOUR TRADES

Another way in which the cash account covers you from debt trouble in the market (never a good thing) is by prohibiting you from purchasing stock from the subsequent proceeds of a sale. That means you can't buy stock now with money you think you're going to make later.

For example, say you invest $100 in XYZ Company stock today, and tomorrow that stock is worth $200, so you sell it. You can't get the $200 you would have made unless you initially had $100 in your account to have made the first trade. "Wait a second," you say. "If you were to have given me the $200 first, and then I were to pay back that initial $100 as if you had loaned it to me, we would all still have come out happy, right?" Let's say for a moment that you bought the $100 worth of XYZ Company stock with borrowed money or a credit line, thinking the value was going to go up, and tomorrow the market tanks and your stock is worth $10. But you've already made a second purchase for ABC Company stock with borrowed money or a credit line, thinking you'll pay it back with the money you're bound to get from the XYZ purchase. Since the original investment never paid off, you're in way over your head.

TIP

Beginning investors should seriously consider opening a cash account that limits any type of financial damage from a bad investment to nothing more than the initial amount invested. While it's not a great idea to purchase stock on credit at any time, it's especially bad for new investors with limited experience.

It's this kind of reasoning that led to the original stock market crash. When the panic forced all stock prices to drop, people were responsible for the amounts of their original trades. Since they didn't actually have that kind of money, they lost their homes, savings, and anything else of value.

If you're convinced that you're a good enough (or lucky enough) investor to avoid these kinds of problems and pitfalls, perhaps you should consider a margin account.

MARGIN ACCOUNT

In a margin account, the brokerage firm basically lends you money. However, you are still required to maintain in your brokerage account at least half the value of the stock that you want to purchase. A margin account enables an investor to make money faster, but be warned: It also enables an investor to lose money faster. The process by which this works is known as *leverage* as discussed earlier in Lesson 6, "Stock Derivatives," whereby additional money or credit is applied to an investor's purchase (or sale) of stock.

PLAIN ENGLISH

Leverage is like a seesaw: The farther you get from the center, the greater the movement. The seats on the seesaw will go higher and lower, as will the value of the investment in larger profits and losses.

Say, for example, that you open a margin account with $1,000. You can place a purchase order for $1,986 worth of XYZ stock. "Wait a second," you say. "Where'd that number come from?" First, we're assuming you're still using the same broker as in the cash account example. You're still required to pay the $7 service charge for the purchase. This leaves you $993 with which to buy the stock. Since you have to maintain at least half the price of the stock purchase, the brokerage can lend you only $993, not $1,000 for the purchase.

$993 + $993 = $1,986

Next, let's say that the value of XYZ stock doubles the next day, and your stock is now worth $3,972 ($1,986 + $1,986). You can sell the stock (the sell order will cost you $7 again), give $993 back to the brokerage house, and pocket $2,972. Compare your $2,972 with the $1,979 the investor with a cash account would have made with the same investment ($993 + $993 = $1,986, which is the initial amount invested and the capital gain when the stock value doubled, minus $7 for the sale is $1,1979), and you're ahead of the other investor by $993.

So why isn't everyone using a margin account? On the other side, let's say you still make the initial purchase of $1,986, and the next day the value of XYZ stock drops by half. Your stock is now worth $993 and that's also the amount the brokerage lent you, so you have to repay that amount plus the $7 for the sale order. You are effectively back at zero. The guy in the cash account, though, is still holding stock worth $496.50 ($993 ÷ 2). Not a great day by any standards, but still preferable to owning nothing and being $7 in debt for service charges to boot.

ONE MORE POINT

Obviously, most real-life examples aren't quite as dramatic or straightforward. Did I mention that the brokerages will also charge you interest on the loan? So even in less dramatic examples, the margin account investor will need to make a higher profit to come out ahead, since the interest charges must be figured into the formula as well.

Finally, certain restrictions apply as to what kinds of stocks can be purchased or sold through margin accounts. These restrictions are usually reserved for the more obscure stocks and therefore don't necessarily prohibit regular day-to-day transactions.

Margin accounts certainly appeal to the risk takers. In addition, they can prove a useful tool for someone who has the resources to back any error, but it is an area best avoided by new investors.

CAUTION

Make sure you directly question your broker about any restrictions before opening a margin account. As with anything dealing with money, make sure you know what you're getting yourself into.

DRIPs

Direct Reinvestment Plans, or DRIPs, are an ingenious method many companies have developed to make their stock available to individual investors without the use of a broker. The company raises capital funds without having to go through the expense and trouble of issuing new stock and the investor makes out by minimizing or avoiding a broker fee altogether through purchasing stock directly from the company. In addition, many companies will even reduce the stock price from its market price.

DRIPs are designed for investors to accumulate stock in the company by requiring subsequent systematic purchases of the stock. To maximize that result, and because purchases and sales of the stock are handled through the company, redeeming or selling your shares may require a substantially longer period of time.

Most of the larger companies such as Home Depot and the Chase Manhattan Bank, for example, offer DRIPs, although few if any are aggressively advertised. Should you firmly believe the potential of a particular company's merits, check its Web site or contact the company through its main number and ask about the availability and particulars of its DRIP program.

THE 30-SECOND RECAP

- The minimum amount required to open a brokerage account varies, as do potential perks.

- A cash account is a brokerage account in which the investor may purchase stock equivalent to no more than the amount of money available.

- A margin account is a brokerage account whereby an investor can purchase stock with money loaned by the brokerage. The amount of the loan cannot exceed the amount of money maintained within the account by the individual investor.

- Direct Reinvestment Plans (DRIPs) are programs offered directly from companies whereby potential investors make systematic purchases of the stock in return for absorbed broker costs and reduced share prices.

LESSON 10

How Much Stock to Buy and How to Buy It

In this lesson you will learn about the appropriate notations and instructions to give a broker to purchase stock on your behalf.

DETERMINING HOW MUCH STOCK TO BUY

So far you know what stock is, you know what a brokerage account is, you have opened either your cash account or your margin account, and you've decided you are ready to buy some stock. Now you need to determine what size trade you wish to purchase. Careful attention and thought in this step can save you a lot of money.

PLAIN ENGLISH

The **size of your order** means the number of shares of stock you wish to trade.

For example, most service charges are per transaction, not per *size of the order.* Thus, a single purchase of 100 shares of XYZ Company at a dollar per share will cost you $107: $100 for the stock and $7 for the purchase order. In contrast, 10 separate purchases of 10 shares of XYZ will cost you $170: $100 for the stock and $7 each for the 10 purchase orders.

You can see how quickly and how dramatically the size of the purchase makes a difference in your profit. In the first example, the value of your stock has to rise by 7 percent before you actually begin to make a profit from your stock purchase. In the second example, the value of the stock has to rise by *70 percent* before you can begin to make a profit. That's going to take a lot longer.

When purchasing stock, you will need to select one of the following two options:

- Round lots
- Odd lots

ROUND LOTS

Because of those expense pitfalls, many investors buy in round lots. Purchasing in round lots is similar to the process of buying beer or soda. You're certainly welcome to buy bottles or cans individually, but most people will pick up a six-pack, right? A *round lot* is a "six-pack" of stock, except that it's not six shares. Round lots usually trade in groups of 100.

PLAIN ENGLISH
A **round lot** is a predetermined number of shares of stock that is standard for purchases and sales—usually 100 shares.

In addition, there are a number of shares that trade in round lots of 10, which are known as *cabinet stocks*. Before you get too excited about cabinet stocks though, you should know that cabinet stocks trade in groups of 10 primarily because of their astronomical share prices. Prices for shares of cabinet stocks (their names are unfamiliar to the average investor) are usually in the range of tens of thousands of dollars and therefore priced out of reach of average investors. This type of stock is usually traded only between high net worth (wealthy) individuals and/or institutions.

In addition to paying fewer service charges and gaining more cost-efficiency, purchasers of round lots usually have the advantage of lower prices per share. This practice sounds a little unfair to the smaller investor because the "richer investors" get lower prices, but it makes more sense when you consider the paperwork and employee time consumed by subsequent purchases rather than one round-lot purchase.

As a smaller investor who wants to buy in round lots, you can do one of two things:

- Keep depositing into your brokerage account until you have enough to buy the round lot.

- Group together with other smaller investors to purchase the round lot.

Should you be fiercely independent or not have any friends, perhaps you should consider purchasing in odd lots.

Should you decide to save money in your brokerage account, be sure and ask what types of financial products are available in which you can park your money until you use it to initiate a trade. Virtually all brokerages offer money-market products such as mutual funds, with which investors can earn interest on money not currently being used. If you don't ask, you run the risk of losing possible interest payments.

TIP

Purchasing stocks in round lots through pooling its members' funds is an advantage investment clubs offer novice investors. Investment clubs also offer opportunities for sounding out new ideas, studying and learning, and networking into the financial community.

ODD LOTS

If a round lot is the "six-pack" of stock purchase, an odd lot is the à la carte of stock purchase. Simply put, an *odd lot* is any trade involving fewer than 100 shares (or fewer than 10 in the case of those cabinet stocks). Although the price per share can be a little higher, odd lots are the preferred method of purchase for many investors.

First of all, you can purchase exactly the number of shares you want; no more, no less. If you want to buy 29, 32, or 61 shares of stock, you don't have to round up to 100, as in a round lot purchase. Second, you can purchase by amount rather than by share. For example, you want to buy $100 worth of XYZ Company stock, and the stock is worth $12 per share. By buying in an odd lot, you can buy 8.3 shares of XYZ stock.

PLAIN ENGLISH

An **odd lot** is any number or shares of stock that are purchased outside of a predetermined standard.

Many investors do buy in odd lots and are unhappy about not getting the price deals available in round lots. As a result, many brokerages have addressed this situation by grouping together their own investors in order to purchase round lots at round lot prices. So, even without friends, you may still be able to get the better price.

DETERMINING HOW TO BUY YOUR STOCK

In virtually every movie I see that has a stock market scene, people are screaming "Buy, sell, limit, stop, market order," and so on at the top of their lungs. (Usually these same people are also involved in substantially more intrigue than ever happens on the stock floor, but that's another matter.) Here we finally get to clear up the confusion regarding the terms used in purchasing and selling stock. Contrary to popular belief, these terms are not interchangeable and they actually do mean something.

After you've decided to buy stock in either a round or an odd lot, you need to tell your broker how to *order* the stock.

PLAIN ENGLISH

> **Orders** are instructions given to a broker to specify under what conditions stock should be bought or sold.

CONSIDER TIMING

Your first consideration is the amount of time in which you allow your broker to complete the transaction for you.

Say that you want your broker to buy 100 shares of XYZ Company, but only if the broker can do it today, because tomorrow, for whatever reason, you don't want him or her to continue to attempt to complete the transaction. This instruction is known as a *day order.* The vast majority of all transactions is done as day orders, partly because, unless the investor specifies that the order should remain open longer, it is assumed to be a day order. Another reason for the preference of day orders is that most people want their transactions performed now, not in the future, because of such factors as market volatility and price fluctuation.

Investors do have the option, however, to keep their order open longer by specifying how long they want the broker to continue to attempt to complete the transaction. The length of time may depend on many factors, such as the lack of availability of the stock or the investor's belief that the price of the stock is about to change. When the order is placed, the investor gives a time limit, or *time notation.* These time notations include ...

GTW. Good **T**hrough the **W**eek means that the order will remain open until the closing time of the last trading day or session of the week.

GTM. Good **T**hrough the **M**onth means that the order will remain open until the closing time of the last trading day or session of the month.

GTC. Good un**T**il **C**anceled means that the order will remain open until the investor instructs the broker to cancel it.

PLAIN ENGLISH

A **time notation** is an instruction to a broker specifying how long an order to purchase or sell stock should remain in effect.

No, I don't know why the last one isn't GUC instead of GTC; it just is. To further confuse the situation, GTC orders are also known as *open orders.* This simply means that the order is open until the investor closes, or cancels, it. That's not so confusing.

CONSIDER PRICE

Next, you have to tell the broker how much you want to pay for the purchase, or at what price you are willing to sell the stock. This is done by giving one of the following orders:

- Market orders
- Limit orders
- Stop orders

MARKET ORDERS

Market orders are the kind most commonly given when purchasing and selling stock. When you place a market order, you simply tell your broker to purchase or sell a certain number of shares. You do not specify the price or time frame within which you consider the purchase or sale acceptable. As discussed previously, the market order is assumed to be a day order, unless specified otherwise. The broker will go to the market, usually within a couple of minutes—or in the case of e-brokerages, seconds—and purchase or sell your stock at whatever price the stock is trading.

PLAIN ENGLISH

> **Market orders,** also know as *open orders,* instruct the broker to go to the market immediately and buy or sell shares at whatever price is currently being offered.

If the order were meant to be fulfilled immediately, would there be any reason for not making it a day order? Could it be anything else? Sometimes stocks may be difficult to sell or to find for purchase at given rates. For example, say you want to buy 100 shares of XYZ Company stock. Remember that XYZ Company issued a limited number of stocks to begin with, so there are really only 105 shares trading on the market. It's going to take your broker a lot longer than a day to track down those 100 shares for you to purchase—if he or she is able to do it at all. In the case of selling, should your stock be unattractive, the broker may not be able to find someone who is willing to purchase it. In either case, you may wish to consider leaving the order open a little longer than a day by using one of the previously discussed notations.

As a side note, the broker doesn't really "go to the market." One thing those Wall Street movies do show realistically is that there are already far too many people on the Exchange floor. In addition, some of those markets aren't physically real, but we'll get into that later. Almost all transactions these days are handled by computerized systems, so your broker is free to conduct your business within the comfort of his or her office.

Limit Orders

Limit orders are perfectly named, as they imply that a limit has been placed on the price the investor is willing to pay to purchase the stock or that a minimum price has been given at which the investor will sell the shares he or she currently owns. In addition, limit orders are always placed at a different price than that at which the stock is currently trading—higher for sales and lower for buys. This is known as *away from the market.*

> **PLAIN ENGLISH**
> **Limit orders** instruct a broker to purchase stock at a price lower than the current market price or to sell stock at a price higher than the current market price.

Let's suppose that you want to buy 100 shares of XYZ Company, which at the moment is trading for $10 per share. You are convinced, because of something you read in the newspaper, that the price of the stock is about to drop—XYZ is being sued for copying ABC Company's patent, let's say. You are an attorney who knows that ABC Company's case won't stand up in court. Therefore, you figure that the initial price of $10 per share of XYZ Company will drop when people get the bad news and then will go up again when people get the later news that the case has been dismissed. You give your broker a *buy limit order.*

The buy limit order tells your broker to purchase XYZ Company's stock *only when it drops to a certain price,* which in your case is $8. You will also probably want to use a notation to tell your broker how long you are willing to wait for the price to drop: a day, a week, or a month. You do this, of course, believing that the value of the stock will eventually go back up. So your investment strategy is to buy as if the stock is on momentary sale.

On the other hand, if you currently own XYZ stock valued at $8 and you believe its price is going to go up and then later drop, you will want to give your broker a *sell limit order.* By doing so, you tell the broker to sell your stock only if the price rises to $10. Of course, you are assuming that the price of XYZ stock will later drop and remain below the price of $10. This is called getting out when the going's good.

CAUTION

Be warned that the type of timing necessary to successfully manipulate limit orders doesn't come quickly or easily. New investors are strongly urged to consider the pitfalls in this type of trading before attempting it.

STOP ORDERS

The other side of the limit order is the *stop order*. By using a stop order, an investor limits fluctuation of the price at which he or she is willing to own the stock. Or, in other words, the stop order is used to keep an investor from losing money he or she has already made on long and short positions.

Long: A long position simply means that an investor owns a share of stock outright and has full rights as pertain to that ownership.

Short: A short position means that an investor has sold stock that he or she has borrowed with the intention of returning the stock by repurchasing it at a later time when the price of the stock has dropped.

Say, for example, that you have already purchased 10 shares of XYZ Company at the price of $10. Luckily, the price of XYZ Company has risen since you purchased it to the price of $20 per share. This is no surprise to you, because you expected the value of the stock to rise, or you wouldn't have purchased the stock to begin with. The stock you purchased that was originally worth $100 is now worth $200. Lucky you!

PLAIN ENGLISH

Using a **stop order,** an investor seeks to cover a short position by instructing a broker to sell stock at a price lower than the current market value or to buy stock at a price higher than the current market value.

But let's also say that you have a sneaking suspicion that the price of XYZ Company will go up for a while and then drop. And, different from the limit order example, you believe that once the price begins to drop, it will not go back up again. You want to protect the $100 profit you have already made. To do this, you give your broker a *sell stop order.* By doing this, you tell your broker, "Should the value of my stock drop below $20 per share, I want you to sell all my stock automatically."

This way, should your stock drop below $20 and you can't get to a phone to yell "Sell! Sell!" as they do in the movies, you're already covered; your broker has received standing instructions from you and should be trying to sell your shares.

You should be aware of three more lines of small print regarding the sell stop order.

1. If you had bought each share of XYZ Company's stock for $10, you obviously couldn't put *a sell stop order* on it for $20, since by definition the stock meets that criterion as soon as you purchase it. To deal with that, most investors give progressively higher sell stop orders as the price of the stock continues to rise. So, upon purchasing the stock, you would place a sell stop order with your broker for, let's say, $9. Once the price of the stock rose to $12, you would place a sell stop order for $11, and so on.

2. If your stock is a volatile one, you could be shooting yourself in the foot without knowing it. As is often the case with volatile stocks, a stock may drop in the morning but rise later in the day. For example, should the price of XYZ drop below

the sell stop order price in the morning, your broker will try to sell it. Should the price jump in the afternoon as everyone notices the price drop and thinks the stock is a bargain, you may lose out on the price increase—because you may no longer own that particular stock, thanks to your extremely efficient broker.

3. In each of these transactions, remember that service charges would apply, and we've discussed how these can quickly eat away any or all the profits you may have actually made with your trading.

A *buy stop order* is a little more complicated since short positions are involved. Should you need a refresher, a short position works like this. Say the price of XYZ Company stock is at $10. You believe the price will go down to $5. A *short position* will allow you to actually *make* money from the decline in the stock price. You would "borrow" 10 shares of XYZ Company and sell them at the price of $10. When (if) the price did actually drop, you would purchase 10 shares at $5, return them to the market where you borrowed them, and pocket the $50 difference.

A buy stop order would function to keep you from losing money in this transaction too. Say you have borrowed and sold the stock, and the price drops to $5. You place a buy stop order with your broker, telling him or her to purchase the 10 shares if the stock price rises to $6. Although you will make less than in the $5 example, the buy stop order will keep you from losing even more if the price of the stock continues to rise. The $40 you pocket by repurchasing the stock at $6 isn't as good as the $50 you would have made by repurchasing the stock at $5, but it's better than the $30 you would have pocketed had the stock risen to $7 and you hadn't had the buy stop order.

All three of the small-print examples regarding the sell stop order also apply to the buy sell order. Successive buy sell orders are required as the price of the stock continues to drop. Minor fluctuations may animate these orders and keep you from making the same profits you would have realized had you sat tight. And those darn service charges keep adding up and adding up.

TIP

Stop orders may possibly limit your ability to make money, but they will definitely protect you from losing money. For this reason they are particularly popular with new investors.

THE 30-SECOND RECAP

- Round lots are the standard number of shares grouped together for trading, usually 100 shares for common stock.

- Odd lots refer to trading shares outside of round lots, that is, piecemeal or individually.

- Time notation refers to an instruction to your broker as to the time frame within which each of the following orders must be filled.

- A market order is a direction to a broker to go to the market immediately and purchase the selected stock at the best price currently available.

- A limit order is a direction to a broker to purchase stock should the price fall from its current price or sell it should the stock price rise.

- A stop order is a direction to a broker to sell stock at a price lower than the current market value or to buy stock at a price higher than the current market value for the purposes of hedging losses or covering a short position.

LESSON 11

How to Pick Stocks

In this lesson you will learn to determine what you want to accomplish by investing, and which stocks are most appropriate to help you reach those goals.

DETERMINING YOUR OBJECTIVES

Now that you have a better understanding of how all the markets work, you're probably ready to invest. Before you put one dime into the market, however, it is imperative that you have a solid idea of what your goals are for investing, how you aim to meet those goals, and what types of investments you consider acceptable in meeting these goals. This is the first step in what is referred to as *investment planning.*

> **PLAIN ENGLISH**
>
> **Investment planning** means determining the goals you hope to achieve by investing and then deciding on the methods and vehicles that will enable you to achieve your goals.

Here are some typical goals that people set for themselves:

- Large-scale purchases—a boat or vacation home
- Current financial security—a good nest egg
- College fund—for yourself or your children

- Preparation for retirement—income to supplement Social Security

Your first step, then, is to determine your goal. It must be a concrete goal, or else how will you know when you've reached it?

Ask 100 people if they want to be rich, and it's a pretty safe bet that 100 will tell you yes. It's also a pretty safe bet that few, if any, of those 100 people are rich. This is because people as a rule tend to think of money in such vague terms as rich, poor, expensive, and cheap. Question these same people further regarding what these terms mean to them, and most will give you a blank stare or give you a vague definition—"Rich means lots of money." But what is a lot of money? It will be difficult to determine when you are "rich" if you have no concept of what rich is.

MEASURING YOUR OBJECTIVE

Thus it is essential that you have a concrete and measurable goal when entering the investment arena, rather than depending on indefinite guidelines or, worse yet, jumping in and hoping for the best.

For example, during my first year as an investor, I made a goal for myself of establishing $10,000 in one year through savings, investments, freelance jobs, etc. I didn't make my goal, but I came close. Two months into the second year, I did finally reach that elusive $10,000 goal. Only by having that measurable goal, however, did I know during the journey to $10,000 how I was doing, when I needed to work a little harder, when I could take a little more risk in my investments, and when I could take a little break. In addition, that measurable $10,000 goal affected my day-to-day life in that I knew when I needed to clip coupons, when I could afford a vacation, and how much of my annual bonus I could spend as opposed to how much I needed to save.

Having that benchmark of $10,000 is what got me, if a little late, to my goal. It is very difficult, if not impossible, to reach a goal without having one. Think of it this way: You are a professional baseball player. You want to improve your batting average to .300, so you stand at the plate and keep swinging the bat … without a ball to hit. In theory, you would certainly improve your swing and therefore your batting average, but without a ball to hit you really have no idea whether you are getting better or, more importantly, whether you are getting closer to your goal of batting .300. Without the ball, it's all guesswork. Investing works on the same principle. You've got to have balls.

BENCHMARKING YOUR GOALS

That $10,000 goal is only one goal on the road to a larger goal of mine, owning a townhouse in Manhattan. When determining your goals, often the end goal is a big one. That is fine, but if your sole goal is one that is going to take some time to achieve, you may get too discouraged and quit before you reach it. Setting up markers along the way in the form of smaller goals will help you measure your progress. In addition, as humans, we often need a little pat on the back for all our hard work, and these more-minor goals will provide frequent pats, rather than having to wait many years for one big pat on the back.

TIP

> Determine at what points and by what methods you will chart your progress toward your goal. This often entails dividing your final goal into smaller, more easily achieved goals.

Individual goals will obviously vary as greatly as the people who make them. They should, however, have a couple of things in common. They should be …

- **Realistic.** Try to buy a townhouse in Manhattan, not Manhattan itself.

- **Measurable.** Pick a specific number; don't just say that you want to be "rich."

- **Part of a larger goal.** Save for the down payment on your boat as part of your larger goal of owning a boat.

- **Fluid, or easily adaptable as your circumstances change.**

KEEPING YOUR GOALS FLUID

That last item is tricky. Remember when I said I didn't make the $10,000 in the first year? "Fluid" means that I took it on the chin and kept trying to reach that goal. I did eventually reach it; it just took an additional two months. I did not, however, throw up my hands, determine my goal unachievable, and blow all my money on a trip to Disneyland. Fluid is also sometimes called the reality factor because reality is often the factor that keeps us from achieving our goals. Rather than dismiss your goal, you might need to alter it slightly. "Okay, I'll amass $10,000 in 14 months instead of 12."

CAUTION

Ensure that your goals remain achievable by being able to adapt to external circumstances. Many people often aim a little high when initially determining their goals. This is not a bad thing, but it can be discouraging to keep aiming for a goal you may not be able to reach. Fluidity ensures you can sometimes lower these goals for that reason, or for extenuating circumstances you may not have been able to predict when determining your goals—the loss of a job, for example.

Fluidity keeps us focused on our goals; it is *not* the excuse for failing to reach them. By the way, the reverse is true too. Had I reached my $10,000 goal in 10 months, my goal would have changed to $12,000 for the year. Don't rest on your laurels—unless you have made a conscious decision to do exactly that.

DETERMINING YOUR VEHICLE

Defining your *trading objective* is a fancy financial way of saying figure out what you want your investments to do. Say that you want them to enable you to buy a boat. But exactly how do you expect your investments to buy that boat—on credit, lump sum, or payments? You need to determine how your investments will enable you to achieve your goal.

PLAIN ENGLISH

Determining your **trading objective** is the process of deciding what you want your investment to accomplish. Your trading objective then becomes an aid in the selection of the appropriate stock.

People who decide they want their investments to supplement their regular income are going to expect their investments to behave substantially different from people who are saving for their retirement. You will need to decide for yourself how each individual stock will contribute to your personal trading objective. Several different types of stock and definitions of how they operate follow:

- Income stocks

- Growth stocks

- Speculative stocks

INCOME STOCKS

PLAIN ENGLISH

Principal means the original amount you invested.

Investors with income objectives expect their investments to provide supplementary income on a regular basis. Often, this is the trading objective of someone or something (an endowment, a foundation) who gets a windfall of cash. Rather than spend the lump sum all at once, the person or entity has decided to invest the cash and regularly withdraw the proceeds, leaving the principal untouched. This is such a common investment strategy that a number of stocks are termed *income stocks* because they are specifically designed to provide investments through, for example, regular or higher dividend payments. In addition, you should be aware that income stocks promise nothing more than higher or more regular dividends. The term in no way implies that the investment is more or less sound than other investments, since income stocks run the gamut from blue chip stocks to junk bonds.

TIP

> If you are looking for additional income, **income stocks** are stocks that provide a higher or more regular dividend payment rather than a substantial capital gain.

GROWTH STOCKS

Growth is almost certainly the most popular as an investment strategy. So much so, in fact, that growth is further broken down into two subcategories: *conservative* and *aggressive.* Growth as a general term implies that the objective of the stock is to increase in value (remember growth stocks from Lesson 5, "The Five Types of Stock"?). These increases, or capital gains, usually imply that the investor has purchased the stock as a long-term investment. The future value of the stock is more important than its current potential. This type of investment is therefore the staple of most education savings, retirement plans, and the like. Growth attempts to make money over a long course of time by reinvesting most or all of the profits and proceeds back into the company to make it more valuable, thereby increasing the value of the stock. Dividends and income are not the major focus.

In the case of *conservative growth,* particular attention is paid to preserving the capital or, in other words, to making sure your investments aren't going to lose the original amount you invested. Conservative growth promotes companies whose value will rise over time while remaining particularly stable. Intel, for example, is a stable company whose existence is almost assured in today's computerized lifestyle. As the world's computer needs increase, the value of Intel should rise, with little concern that the company will ever go out of business or suffer such heavy losses that the value of the stock would fall below your original investment amount. By the way, this is not a plug for Intel … no one ever thought Pan Am would go out of business either.

Aggressive growth should be obvious, and except for the unspoken pitfalls it is. *Aggressive growth* is growth that is, well, more aggressive than conservative. Obviously, growth-oriented investors want their stocks to increase in value, and the more the better, so why would anyone not choose aggressive? It is a generally accepted rule in investing that the higher the return, the higher the risk. We will discuss risk in greater detail later in this lesson, but think of it in sky-diving terms. The higher up you go before jumping, the greater the thrill. But, the higher up you go, the greater your chances of a mishap on the way down. Aggressive growth works on that same principle. Aggressive growth stocks are therefore usually those that produce faster growth, at the expense of the security of your principal. You might make more, but you run a higher risk of losing it all.

PLAIN ENGLISH

Conservative growth stocks focus on increasing capital gains of the stock but not at the expense of losing capital. **Aggressive** growth stocks focus on increasing capital gains of the stock and are willing to accept higher principal risk to achieve this growth.

SPECULATIVE STOCKS

It is not an accident that Las Vegas is one of America's most popular tourist destinations. People love a good gamble. *Speculative stocks* provide the opportunity for stout-hearted investors to do just that in the investment market. There are two different schools of thought on what constitutes a speculative stock, but their differences are minimal.

> **CAUTION**
> Always keep in mind that speculative stocks have little or no real value other than unsupported potential; that is, they are long shots.

The first school of thought defines a speculative stock as one that the investor has purchased for a short-term gain. As an investment strategy, this is frowned upon, particularly for new investors. Honestly speaking, the ability to choose a stock that will rise significantly in a short period of time is a skill that most newer investors simply haven't honed. In all fairness, however, even seasoned investors often get burned with these types of investments. Even though stories in the newspapers portray "day traders" as computerized whiz kids who make millions of dollars per day, the reality is significantly different. Should you decide that this investment strategy appeals to you, seriously ensure you know what you are getting yourself into. Always remember, when someone's making money, it's got to come from somewhere. More often than not, it's coming from the person on the other side of the desk who just lost it.

The second school of thought defines a speculative stock as a stock that has little or no real value but has the potential for great gains. Do you remember hearing about junk bonds in the 1980s? That's an excellent example, even though they were bonds, not stock. Bonds, or rather I should say the companies who issue bonds, get credit ratings just like you and me. When the bond's credit rating is really bad (below a "B"), the company is so unlikely to pay the money owed to the bondholder that the bond is considered "junk." Stocks work on the same principle.

Remember the blue chip stocks from Lesson 5? Those companies are solid, with no real fears of going out of business; whereas on the other end of the spectrum are those companies that have started out with a couple of quarters and a shoestring. These companies can't justify an investment in themselves, because they own little of real value (what's a shoestring really worth?). However, any one of these companies might turn out to be the next Microsoft, Iomega, or Coca-Cola; or they might simply go belly up, in which case you would lose your total investment. This concept differs from the other definition of speculative investing in that you could still be buying the stock for the long term, expecting that the world wasn't yet clamoring for whatever product or service the company provided, only because the product or service (or the company for that matter) was still new and/or undiscovered.

While this scenario is the dream of all investors (who wouldn't have liked to have bought Microsoft when it first went public?), it's rare enough in its most basic form that those who buy these types of stocks (short-term-gain earners or extensive-capital-gain earners) are often referred to as "speculators" rather than investors. Hint: These types of investments are "long shots," not the well-researched, well-thought-out types of investments you and I are aiming for.

DETERMINING YOUR ACCEPTABLE LEVEL OF RISK

Determining your investment strategy will largely depend on your stomach for risk. *Risk* is the probability that you will lose the original amount you put into the investment. Notice the qualifier "original amount." As a rule, if you lose all your profits and wind up back with the original amount you invested, for investing purposes you've broken even. Although that scenario would be a pretty pathetic investment by anyone's standards, it is still better than losing everything, including the original amount invested.

TIP

It's important to determine the level of risk you are willing to accept. Decide what the risks are to your investment, evaluate these risks, and decide whether or not you are prepared to accept the risks.

Think of the concept of risk and return as a footrace in which stocks are the runners and the course has lots of potholes. All the stocks are trying to make their way to the finish line (payoff). The younger, lighter, less-established stocks certainly move faster toward the finish line, but they stand substantially more chance of getting tripped up by a pothole. The older, heavier, and more established stocks don't move as quickly, but when those potholes come up it's going to take a pretty deep one to make the stock slow down, and an even deeper one to make the stock stop altogether.

So why bother to take chances at all? Because risk and return are directly correlated to one another. The less risk you take, the less chance you have to make a profit, or capital gain, as depicted in the following illustration:

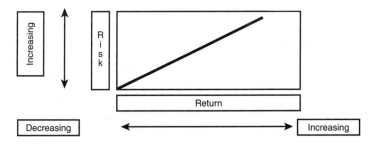

The relationship between risk and return.

On the far left is the kind of return that is absolutely safe, such as putting the money under your mattress rather than investing it. Notice that this return is at the bottom of the risk indicator, or the left side of the table—this means no risk. Handling your money this way ensures that you will never lose it—at least not in the stock market. Notice also that the line is at the bottom of the gradual rise indicating return. This means there is also no return on your money. After all, mattress companies don't pay interest on the money you stuff into their products. You would be better off putting that money into the mattress company's stock.

Here's the catch … stock investments don't really work this way, not in direct correlation, anyway. There are those investments that have no practical risk to speak of. For example, if you invested in a U.S. Government Treasury bond, you would still earn a little interest, say 5 to 6 percent. The risk of losing your money would be little, if any, because those bonds are backed by the full faith of the U.S. Government. I suppose the U.S. Government could go out of business, but if it did, you'd have bigger problems than your investments to think of. So, you're making some return, with no "practical risk."

In addition, stories abound about the other side of the coin: those highly risky investments that didn't pay off at all and that, quite truthfully, never stood a chance from the beginning. My brother hits me up all the time with such gems as a company that has developed the first oatmeal-powered car, the launch of television's 24-hour Golf Network, and instant beer (just add water!).

KNOWLEDGE REDUCES RISK

The hard-and-fast rules of risk versus return aren't quite true. That being the case, it would appear that all bets are equal in the case of risk. A big, solid company might just skyrocket in value, while (quite often) a risky company goes out of business and its investors lose everything instead of making fortunes. Fortunately, this also is not the case. The power to determine risk isn't in any set formula but rather in *what you know about what you are getting into.* For example, as much as I like beer, the prospect of powdered beer just doesn't appeal to me. In my mind, I wouldn't buy it, so I'll assume that no one else will either and therefore I won't invest in my brother's recommendation.

On the other side of the coin, AOL was already an established company when it decided to merge with Time Warner. Although AOL was one of those "big companies" mentioned earlier, it would be safe to assume that any growth from AOL stock would be minimal, since the risk of AOL going out of business anytime soon is also minimal. However, events proved that this simply wasn't the case, because the merger drove the price of AOL through the roof.

As a side note, the rumor that mergers always make the price of a stock shoot through the roof isn't necessarily true either.

TIP

> It is generally accepted that when two companies merge, the price of the bigger company's stock will initially drop while the stock price of the company being overtaken will go up. The price of the newly combined stock is expected to rise after that, making the stock particularly attractive to investors.

But the power to determine the amount of risk and return in any investment rests solely on the investor's shoulders and is directly related to the amount of research he or she is willing to make before investing. Therefore, make sure you know all the risks of any investment you are considering. In addition to the basic risk of the company going out of business, several other risks are particularly insidious and should also be considered. The most common risks for you to consider regarding your own potential investment are …

- Inflationary risk
- Political/governmental risk
- Market risk

INFLATIONARY RISK

We are all too familiar with inflation. However, most people are unaware of how inflation can negate an investment. Say you have

$100 and think you might want to purchase a stereo. The stereo you can get for $100 is kind of nice, but what you've really got your eye on is the stereo that costs $150. You decide to invest that $100 and wait until you make $50 in capital gains, at which time you will withdraw the $50 as well as the original $100 and purchase the stereo (let's skip the broker fees for this example). Then, let's say it takes six months for your stock to *appreciate*.

PLAIN ENGLISH

To **appreciate** means to increase in number or value and thus become more valuable.

But, in the time it has taken your $100 to turn into $150, inflation has driven the price of the two stereos to $200 and $250, respectively. You are worse off than had you not invested and just bought the cheaper stereo. True, you've got $150, which is still $50 more than you had, but that won't buy any kind of stereo now. That's *inflation risk*. For the record, since the stock market is driven by the economy, stocks carry the lowest inflation risk of any type of investment.

CAUTION

The **risk of inflation** means that your investment will not maintain its initial purchasing power because it is not growing as fast as the inflation rate.

POLITICAL/GOVERNMENTAL RISK

The American government is about as stable as can be. Other governments around the world aren't quite as lucky, however, and the strange things that foreign governments do can absolutely affect stock investments. The most obvious risk is to those investors who have invested in stock markets in other countries, but the effects of *political* and *governmental risk* go way beyond direct cause and effect.

For example, say you have invested in the good old American Widget Company because you don't want to deal with the headaches of international investing. You don't care that the government of North Svengobia has just sealed its borders to all trade with the United States over a territorial dispute. Did I mention that North Svengobia is the only country in the world where the Widget flower, which is so important in the production of Widgets, grows?

PLAIN ENGLISH

Political and **governmental risk** is the danger that decisions by governments over which you have no control will have ramifications that will affect your stock domestically.

This is a very real example. There were some very unhappy pistachio nut investors in the United States when Iran stormed the U.S. embassy in the 1970s, effectively destroying all diplomatic relations with the United States and severing a supply line of pistachio nuts. Other examples of political and governmental risk that would affect American investors include unstable exchange rates, nationalization of industries, and trade agreements such as NAFTA. As increasing globalization causes our world to continue to shrink, the power of governmental and political risk will only grow larger.

MARKET RISK

Market risk comes in two parts. The first part of market risk lies in the interdependence of all stocks. Although it is true that the value of each stock is independent, the reality is that all stocks in the market share one thing in common—they are all on the market together. As such, it is impossible to disregard the effect that the overall movement of the market has on your individual stock.

PLAIN ENGLISH

Market risk is the danger that your stock's performance will be skewed as a result of the conditions of
the markets in which it trades.

This effect means that, to some extent, when the entire market goes
up, your stock probably will too; and when the entire market goes
down, your stock probably will too. This rule isn't set in stone. Some
investors make a killing on the same day others are losing their shirts,
but realistically the movement of the market is nothing more than a
summary of the movement of the stocks within it. Finding a stock that
behaves differently from the rest of the market, then, is going to be
very difficult to do.

The risk here is that while your stock may be well thought out, in a
really good company, and ready to grow, the pull of the market,
should it go down, could be strong enough to take your stock with it.
Think of it like all those lifeboats floating around after the *Titanic*
went down. They were floating fine on their own; it was the pull of
the *Titanic* that sucked them under.

The second part of market risk lies in trying to sell your stock. When
the market is spiraling down, quite frankly, there aren't a whole lot of
people who are looking to get in. While conventional wisdom holds
that this is exactly the time people should be getting into the market,
few do. As a result, you may have a very difficult time trying to sell
your stock. This is referred to as an *illiquid market*.

TIP

An **illiquid market,** or a market in which few people
are buying and/or selling stock, usually occurs when
stock prices are shooting up or plummeting down. If
prices are plummeting, it's a good time to buy more
stock.

Attempting to sell your stock under these conditions usually means that you will have to pay larger transaction fees, reduce the price you will accept for the stock, or anything else you can think of to make your stock more attractive to potential buyers. This, of course, means a loss of money to you.

THE 30-SECOND RECAP

- Determining your investment objectives includes determining what you want your stock to accomplish, and which stocks will best achieve that goal.

- Ensure that you pick realistic, measurable goals which are part of a larger goal and still able to change when necessary.

- Examples of the different types of stock include: income stocks that focus on paying out profits in larger regular dividend payments, growth stocks that reinvest most or all of their profits into the corresponding company to provide higher capital gains, and speculative stocks that have little or no real value, but offer the possibility of high returns through high risk.

- Risk and return is the concept by which your potential for profit rises and falls in direct proportion to the potential to lose money. You must determine where on the spectrum you want your investments.

- Different types of risk you should consider include: Inflation risk, which means that your profits won't stay ahead of the inflation rate, politial and governmental risk, which include repercussions over domestic and political decisions, and market risk, which includes conditions in the market over which you have no control.

LESSON 12
Evaluating Stocks

In this lesson you will learn the mathematical formulas necessary to effectively evaluate and research your stock's performance and what they measure and mean.

THE DREADED MATH PART MADE EASY

Stocks are financial instruments, and financial instruments are measured numerically. At some point, then, your stock selection is going to have to include math if it is to be a sound investment choice. Most financial documents regarding stock are packed with ratios and equations. This, in addition to all the fine print with such comments as "These securities have not been approved by the SEC" is enough to frighten the most stout-hearted investors into running back to their mattresses to hide their money.

Here's the catch: You don't need to understand most of those figures in order to get a good idea of how good a stock is. Highly technical statistical information is available should you need or want to see it, but getting quite so much information on a stock is probably overkill for the average investor.

TIP

Analyze the past performance and project the future performance of stocks that interest you by using statistics and formulas.

Think of analyzing a stock as betting on a baseball game. You could just pick your favorite team, but it would probably be a better bet if you knew how your team (stock) had done in its last game against the same team. It would be an even better bet if you knew how your team had played the whole season leading up to that game. You could learn who is playing on the team (the fund managers), what the weather's going to be like (market conditions), and who has the home field advantage (how the stock performed in this type of market before). At some point, however, the sheer amount of numerical information, from comparative batting averages of individual team members to the laws of probability, would become unmanageable for anyone save maybe a statistician or bookie.

Stock is no different. You will need to at least become familiar with the following indicators of stock health, but information above and beyond this probably isn't necessary to an individual investor:

- Price/earnings ratio
- Earnings per share
- Current/dividend yield
- Current and debt ratios
- Book value
- Credit ratings

As a side note, I work in a bank, and I'm still not familiar with all of the mass of statistics that crosses my desk. I do, however, attempt to learn what is being determined by an equation as I am made aware of it. As an investor, make it a point to try to become increasingly familiar with the "financial stuff." While it may not be essential, it will make you a better-informed investor.

THE PRICE/EARNINGS RATIO

The *price/earnings ratio* is a measurement of how much income the investor can expect from the initial investment. It is measured by dividing the price of the stock by the amount of money the stock issued (or is expected to issue) in dividends over a 12-month period:

Current Market Price of Stock: $10

÷ Earnings over 12-Month Period: $1

= Price/Earnings Ratio: 10

Thus, $10 ÷ $1 = 10.

PLAIN ENGLISH

> The **price/earnings ratio** is the ratio of a stock's current price relative to its earnings over a determined period of time.

The *current market price* of the stock is the amount for which the stock is currently trading. In the preceding example, to buy a share of that stock today would cost $10. The *earnings* are the total of the dividends paid by the stock over a 12-month period. Since dividends are usually paid quarterly, in the same example we know that the total of the four dividend payments was $1. (Let's say that the dividend was $.25 each quarter: .25 + .25 + .25 + .25 = $1.00.) Finally, although in theory you are free to choose any 12-month period you like, there are three 12-month periods that are used most and are generally accepted as providing the best representation of the stock's past performance and future potential. They are described in the next three sections.

THE TRAILING P/E RATIO

The *trailing P/E ratio* uses the dividends of the four quarters of the previous year, regardless of when in the current year the ratio is determined. For example, on January 1, 2000, you would use the dividend payments of the four quarters of 1999 to determine the trailing P/E ratio. On December 31, 2000, you would still use the dividend payment of the four quarters of 1999 to determine the P/E ratio. For that reason, the trailing P/E ratio is most heavily affected by the price of the stock. Because the sum of the four quarters of 1999 never changes, all volatility in the trailing P/E ratio would be as a result of the change in the price of the stock. Comparing the P/E ratio at the end of the year to the P/E ratio at the beginning of the year will indicate whether the quality of the stock's P/E ratio is improving or declining.

THE STANDARD P/E RATIO

The *standard P/E ratio,* or simply the P/E ratio, is the most commonly used ratio, since it provides the most up-to-date, and therefore the most accurate, picture of the stock's current P/E ratio. The (standard) P/E ratio is determined by using the dividends of the last four quarters. For example, if you were determining the P/E ratio on January 1, 2000, you would use the four quarters of 1999. If you were determining the P/E ratio on December 31, 2000, however, you would use the three previous quarters of 2000 and the final quarter of 1999. Because the sum of the previous four quarters would change, as would the daily price of the stock, this P/E ratio is the most volatile, but it is that volatility which enables this P/E ratio to adapt more quickly and thereby to more accurately reflect the health of the stock at that moment.

THE FORWARD P/E RATIO

The *forward P/E ratio* uses the dividends of the previous two quarters and the projected earnings for the next two quarters. For example, if you were determining the P/E ratio on January 1, 2000, you would add the total of the dividends paid in the final two quarters of 1999 and then add what the company believed it would be paying out in the first two quarters of 2000. The projected earnings are used to give a better idea of how the stock's P/E ratio is expected to perform. The use of the trailing two quarters keeps the forward P/E ratio reasonable. A company is going to have a hard time convincing investors that the stock will pay $10 in dividends in the next two quarters if the last two quarters showed dividends of only $1 per share. However, since no one can predict for certain how the stock really will do, the forward P/E ratio gives the least accurate picture of the stock.

INTERPRETING THE P/E RATIO

Now that you know the parts that determine the P/E ratio, what does it measure in real terms? Think of it this way: Say you want to buy a store. You find both a clothing store and a convenience store for sale. To buy the clothing store will cost you $1,000, and you know that the store generates $100 in profits per year. The convenience store will cost you $2,000 but will generate $250 per year in profit. The clothing store will generate $1 in profit for every $10 of your investment. The convenience store, however, will make $1 for every $8 you put into it ($1,000 \div 100 = 10:1$ versus $2,500 \div 200 = 8:1$). While the convenience store is more expensive, it is obviously a better investment. Stocks work on the same principle in that a P/E ratio doesn't concern itself with how much or how little a stock costs, but rather with what kind of return you can expect for the investment—in other words, how much bang-for-your-buck potential.

TIP

Since the P/E ratio is a fraction of the price of the stock, investors refer to a P/E ratio as trading for X times earnings: "Krispy Kreme is trading at 10 times earnings." This means that the stock price of Krispy Kreme is 10 times its dividends over the last 12 months.

As a very general rule, normal P/Es average between 10 and 20 times earnings. This rule will disappear quickly as you look at today's stock markets. Computer companies that are expected to continue to grow are carrying P/E loads of up to 100 times earnings today and are still considered valuable investments. Anything over 20 times earning is still considered a "high P/E ratio," however, regardless of whether the high ratio can be justified or not. High P/E ratios are therefore generally considered to be the terrain of growth companies and companies with the potential for currently unrealized gains.

Anything under 10 is considered a "low P/E ratio." These are usually considered the territory of those big, established blue chip companies, or a company that for whatever reason isn't expected to grow very much. Like anything else subject to risk and return, these big, established companies might not deliver the highest bang for the buck. However, the security of the investment may be more important to the investor than the potential for growth offered by a stock with a higher P/E.

EARNINGS PER SHARE

Earnings per share, or EPS, is a fancy financial way of saying "divided amounts." The total amount of a company's net earnings divided by the number of outstanding common shares is the earnings per share. The EPS determines the stock's dividends in dollars and cents.

PLAIN ENGLISH

Earnings per share is the amount of the dividends paid per share of stock owned.

The EPS is determined by adding up the number of dividends paid over a specific period of time, usually a year or four quarters, or simply the amount paid in one particular dividend payment. For all its simplicity, however, the earnings per share is hands-down the most popular measure of a stock's health. Its simplicity makes the EPS easy to understand and makes it a straightforward indicator of the stock's performance.

In addition to having the flexibility to determine a stock's performance over varying time frames, the resulting EPS can be used any number of ways to determine a stock's health. Three of the most common follow:

1. The EPS of one stock can be compared with the EPS of another stock for the same period. Say you want to invest in AT&T. It would probably be a good move to check out the EPS of other similar stocks, such as MCI or Sprint, to get a better idea of how AT&T has performed within the industry.

2. The EPS of a stock can be compared with itself over a different time frame. Comparing your stock's current EPS with its EPS for the same quarter of the previous year will give you a better idea of the stock's growth or decline over a longer period. This method is therefore more often used for stock that will potentially be held long term.

3. A stock's EPS can be charted over a designated time frame. Comparing the EPS of a stock over the previous four quarters, for example, will highlight changes in the stock's performance and enable you to determine ongoing trends. This type of information can be used to anticipate quick or systematic gains or losses in the next period or quarter.

CAUTION

When comparing the EPS of different stocks, make sure that the method of determining the dividend is the same. Some companies consider only common stock when determining their EPS; others consider options, warrants, and rights, in addition to common stock. This method is called **fully diluted earnings.**

As a final note on the earnings per share, be aware that it is all too easy to mistake the movements of the EPS as Up = good, Down = bad. This is not always the case. The EPS can rise or fall for any number of reasons other than growth in the company.

For example, since the EPS is determined by dividing all the money allotted for dividend payments by the number of common shares outstanding, a company can raise its EPS by reducing the amount of stock outstanding. The resultant rise of the EPS then creates a deceptive picture of the stock's growth. This is a common occurrence with companies that are buying back their own stock.

For that same reason, an EPS might decline while the overall financial health of the company was improving. An EPS might drop, for example, because of a stock split, because the company converted its outstanding bonds and/or preferred stock, or because the company issued rights or warrants. In each of these cases, the EPS of the company would drop independently of the real financial condition of the company.

It is important, then, to remember that although an EPS is a relatively simple tool for measuring a company's growth potential and financial health, that same simplicity offers other investors and companies the option to use different numbers to determine an EPS. Be sure you are all reading from the same page.

TIP

The mass of statistical information about stocks isn't millions of different equations that must all be memorized, but rather it's much of the same information presented in different forms to highlight different aspects of the same stock.

CURRENT/DIVIDEND YIELD

The *current* or *dividend yield* indicates the percentage represented by the annual dividend payments relative to price of the stock. In other words, how much money did you make from your investment (your investment being the stock you purchased)? If this type of measurement is sounding vaguely familiar, that is because the current yield is the exact opposite of the P/E ratio. In fact, the formula to determine the current yield is to flip the P/E ratio formula upside down:

Earnings over 12-Month Period: $1

÷ Current Market Price of Stock: $10

= Current Yield: .10%

Thus, $1 ÷ $10 = .10.

Stocks with high current yields are typically large blue chip stocks, or other stocks with limited growth potential, making them particularly attractive to investors looking for steady income streams from their stock. Since these companies have limited growth potential, most of their profits are paid out to their investors, rather than being reinvested in the company for such things as expansion or research and development. Stocks with low current yields are usually reinvesting their profits, leaving little if anything to pay out to their investors. Logically, then, low current yields are the terrain of growth stocks, which an investor would purchase for anticipated capital growth rather than a steady income stream.

PLAIN ENGLISH

Current yield depicts the dividend payment of a stock as a percentage of the stock's market price. A current yield is the opposite of a P/E ratio.

It is important, as with any measurement, to ensure that you know the baseline from which the measurement is being generated. Simply because a current yield is high or low is not an absolute indicator of anything. Remember that the current yield formula is totally dependent on the amount of dividends paid and that amount is the arbitrary decision of a company's management. That's right; no company is obligated to pay any certain amount in dividends. A company in very bad financial health might decide to pay out 90 percent of all profits in dividends, whereas a company with excellent prospects may decide to pay out only 10 percent of its profits in dividends, choosing to reinvest the balance in expansion. In these cases, the current yield would then give an inaccurate picture of the company. The current yield is still an excellent tool with which to measure a company's financial success and potential. The investor must use the current yield within the context of all its background information for maximum results.

CURRENT AND DEBT RATIOS

The *current ratio* and the *debt ratio* differ from the previous measurements in that their focus is more on the company's constitution rather than its health. This means that the current and debt ratios measure the internal infrastructure of the company, including its level of leverage and its solvency potential, rather than its external dealings.

PLAIN ENGLISH

Current ratio is a projection of the company's ability to meet its financial obligations and otherwise remain solvent. **Debt ratio** is a projection of the total debt carried by a company as compared with the assets and cash flows it maintains.

Think of it this way. Say you make $100,000 a year, and your brother makes $50,000 a year. However, you've got substantially more debt on credit cards than he does (probably because you didn't read Lesson 3, "How Much Do You Have to Invest?" as well as you should have). He's carrying about $5,000 in debt, or about 10 percent, while you've racked up about $50,000, or about 50 percent. It doesn't take a genius to figure out that I'm going to be a lot more comfortable lending your brother money rather than you, for a number of reasons:

1. He's obviously managing his money better than you are (better management). Thus, I'm convinced he's going to handle my (loaned) money more responsibly than you will.

2. He's got a much lower debt *percentage* to carry than you do. All other things being equal (for both of you, rent = 25 percent of your take-home pay, food = 20 percent of your take-home pay, etc.), you are paying a higher relative loan percentage, even though you are also making more money. And struggling to make debt payments of 50 percent is *really* struggling.

3. I've got a better chance of getting some of my money back from your brother should both of you go out of business or, in this case, declare bankruptcy. Remember again that we're working on percentages here. Remembering that taxes, fees,

etc., are usually based on a percentage rather than the amount, your brother would be liable for only about 10 percent of his total income; whereas you would be liable for half. I'll take my chances with your brother.

So the formula to determine the current ratio is ...

Assets ÷ Liabilities = Current Ratio

This current ratio would indicate the probability that in the case of insolvency (bankruptcy), the investor would get all or some of his or her money back after all debts, bonds, and preferred stock were paid off.

On the flip side, the formula to determine the debt ratio is ...

Amount Owed to All Outstanding Bonds

÷ The Company's Total Capitalization

= Debt Ratio

This debt ratio would indicate the company's ability to meet the payments of the debt it carries, or how close the company is to bankruptcy. Using this ratio together with the current ratio, an investor can determine how close the company is to bankruptcy and what the chances are of recovering his or her investment, should bankruptcy occur. Although finding out a company's debt ratio may seem a pessimistic attitude to take, it's certainly better to know this type of information before making your investment rather than after the fact.

Again, remember that these formulas are useful only to the extent that they are used within their respective contexts. That 10-20 rule for high and low ends still applies as it did with the P/E ratios. However, this figure is going to vary widely, depending on the industry. Some companies, such as those that deal with intellectual property such as computer operating systems like Microsoft Windows, will automatically have fewer tangible assets, creating a low debt ratio (under 20 percent), even though they still might be an excellent investment. Other companies, such as manufacturing firms like GM which produces automobiles, may carry high debt ratios (over 30 percent) owing to the amount of infrastructure required to produce their goods, and yet be teetering on the brink of insolvency. In other words, learning a company's current and debt ratios isn't enough: You have to learn *what they mean.*

Book Value

Having learned how to determine the odds of a company going bankrupt, and the odds of its investors being able to get some or all of their investment back, the next logical question is, "How much will I get back?" Fortunately, the book value will tell you just that, or at least give a reasonable estimate. Similar to the way book values are used in the world of buying and selling secondhand cars, a stock's *book value* attempts to determine the worth of a company. Once the book value is known, analysts can subtract the company's liabilities and divide the remainder by the total number of shareholders to determine how much each investor would receive in the case of the company going out of business.

PLAIN ENGLISH

> **Book value** is a simplistic measurement of the total value of a company. It is determined by adding up the values of all tangible assets.

I am not going to give you the formula for determining the book value, because it is one of those statistics that requires spreadsheets, algebraic calculations, and a Ph.D. in mathematics. Suffice it to say that, like any of the preceding measurements, the book value should be used in context with book values of other stocks within the same industry, as well as the same stock's own previous performance.

In addition, the book value has another use. Investors routinely compare the book value with the current market price of the stock to determine how far away from its actual value the stock is trading. As a very general guideline, stocks typically trade at one to two times their book value. Higher book values are certainly more desirable. However, I can't stress enough that, by themselves, these measurements may not necessarily accurately depict the company. You're going to have to do your homework. The more you learn, the better your investment decisions will be.

CREDIT RATINGS

In the current and debt ratio example, we discussed how much debt you and your brother were carrying and how effectively you were each handling it. As individuals, much of this information about you would be available by means of a credit report to anyone who was entitled to see it. With the information on a credit report, entities like mortgage banks and car lease companies can determine whether or not you or your brother would meet their specific minimal criteria.

Wouldn't it be a great world if someone would step in and figure out that kind of stuff for you in the stock market? Luckily for you, a number of companies do exactly that. Stocks, like people, get assigned a *credit rating,* and that credit rating can be used to determine any number of things, including whether or not you choose to purchase that stock as an investment. Such companies as Moody's and Standard and Poor assign these credit ratings, which are available in most newspapers and on the Internet. The credit ratings for stock are a little more detailed since they measure substantially more, but most break down into nine categories using combinations of *A*s, *B*s, and *C*s as demonstrated in the following table.

PLAIN ENGLISH

Credit ratings are evaluations by disinterested parties and services regarding the financial health of a company.

Standard & Poor	Moody's	Fitch	Rating
AAA	Aaa	AAA	The Best
AA	Aa	AA	Very Good
A	A	A	Pretty Good
BBB	Baa	BBB	Good
BB	Ba	BB	So-So
B	B	B	Bad
CCC	Caa	CCC	Pretty Bad
CC	C	CC	Very Bad
C		C	Are You Nuts?

There's no D, DD, or DDD since you can't *more* its bankrupt. Once a company reaches the "D" stage by going bankrupt, its rating gets dropped as you can't give a rating to a company that's out of business.

Frankly, few of us enjoy math, but as you can see, through its use you can uncover a substantial amount of incredibly valuable information. As finance, investment, and money are all measured numerically, numbers will provide the best overall picture of a stock's performance. In addition, the number of formulas you need to extract the most representative view are neither complicated nor many in number. For these reasons, the math part of your stock research should never be minimized or avoided. The time and effort you invest in your research will directly pay off in the potential for your cash investment to flourish.

THE 30-SECOND RECAP

- Researching stock through the use of math will enable you to project its future performance by viewing its past performance. The amount of math necessary to do this is minimal and the formulas required are not complicated.

- Price-to-earnings ratios are one of three percentages determined by comparing the current market of the stock to its dividends over the last four calendar quarters (trailing), the preceding four actual quarters (standard), or the last two actual quarters and two future projected quarters.

- The earnings per share formula enables you to determine the amount of the stock's dividend by dividing the total amount of the issuing company's net earnings by the total number of outstanding common shares.

- Current/dividend yields measure the percentage of the stock's annual divided payments as compared to its market value. This information will enable you to determine how much profit the stock has made as a percentage of its initial purchase cost.

- Current ratio is a measurement of how likely and how much an investor would be able to recoup in the case of a company's insolvency (bankruptcy). It is determined by dividing a company's assets by it's liabilities.

- Debt ratios are a measurement of how near or far a company's relative worth places it toward bankruptcy. It is computed by dividing the company's debt by its assets.

- Book values are a measurement of the total value of a company. It is computed by a highly complicated formula which adds up everything—including intangible items such as name recognition—a company owns.

- Credit ratings are evaluations of the value and ability of companies to repay their debts and produce future earnings. They are performed by professional disinterested parties such as Moody's and Standard and Poor.

Lesson 13
Choosing a Strategy

In this lesson you will learn about methods used to determine how to put together your own customized investment portfolio.

Investment Strategies

Still with me? Okay, you've decided what you want to accomplish by investing, and you know what kind of stocks you are looking for. You have a handle on the potholes that can hold you back, and you've learned how to number-crunch to analyze a stock's performance. You have one step left: deciding how you will apply all this knowledge to your investments. This is both the easiest and the most difficult step of all.

Think of it as buying a car. You've done your research: You've compared the prices at other dealers, you've checked the prices of comparable cars. You've checked the car sales market to find out how this brand is selling and when the best time to buy one is. You've even spoken to prior customers to learn just how the salesmen here haggle. What's your initial offer for the car going to be? How much will you accept for payments? What options do you want in the car? It's time to start making some real choices.

An *investment strategy* is rarely black-and-white. Instead, investment strategies are usually a mix of the different options available. My own experience has been that as my portfolio grows, my investment options grow in direct proportion. In addition, the number of investment strategies represented in my portfolio grows, also in direct proportion. Investment strategies, like investment objectives, should remain fluid in order to adapt to the different circumstances in which you will find yourself, as well as to accommodate any new ideas you yourself will come up with.

Picking an **investment strategy** is the process of determining what information will be most important in your stock selection, how many of each stock you will purchase, and even how and through whom you will purchase that stock.

An exhaustive list of investment strategies is impossible because they are as individual as the people who employ them. Stories circulate about people who pick their investments by using dart boards, astrology, and (so I've heard) even monkeys. As a new investor, however, you should be aware of some of the more popular (and saner) methods people employ for investing in their stocks:

- The recommendation strategy

- The research strategy

- Buy and hold

- Dollar cost averaging

- Constant dollar averaging

Mix and match as you see fit; take what you want and leave what you don't like. In the world of investing, the only right answer is yours.

RECOMMENDATIONS

When people learn you have begun your investment career, "experts" will begin to crawl out of the woodwork. In all fairness, a significant number of *recommendations* you receive will have true merit. People who discuss the companies they work for are certainly in a better position to discuss their internal structures than the average person on the street.

TIP

> A **recommendation** is advice or information, some-
> times unsolicited, received from other people who
> may possibly have better insight into the stock than
> you do.

Furthermore, your friends and family may be able to provide real
insight into a company and its products and services with which you
may be unfamiliar. When deciding whether to invest in Home Depot,
for example, I asked a friend of mine who is an engineer to tell me of
his experiences with them. I write financial books; I couldn't hang
drywall if it came up and introduced itself to me. After our discussion,
however, I felt much better about my final decision.

I asked my brother for much the same kind of information before
making an investment in a video game stock. I don't play video
games, but he does extensively. My discussions with him enabled me
to make an intelligent decision about which games were hot, which
systems had problems, and what innovations were being anticipated
by consumers.

The other side of the coin is best illustrated by a great commercial
currently running on television. A young guy walks up to a very dis-
tinguished gentleman in an art gallery and whispers to him, "I over-
heard your stock recommendation last week and put all my money in
XYZ stock." The older gentleman replies, "Good for you. They will
be the only company authorized to produce Widgets once the Martians
take control of Earth," as his nurse leads him back to the home.

The moral is obvious: Recommendations are a wonderful source of
information as long as you know their source and the recommender's
expertise on the subject.

TIP

Which recommendations merit further research and which are duds? Ask the recommender, "Why do you recommend this company?" If the person has a concrete reason (personal experience with the stock, product, or service), I'll look into it. If the person answers, "Someone told me it was a good investment," it's a dud.

RESEARCH

Research is a vague term, and it could include pretty much anything. Asking people to share their experiences is research, so is requesting a copy of the company's annual report. Checking the general press is research, as is digging up evaluations of the stock on the Internet. As a result, a precise definition of "research," one that applies to every stock and/or investor, is difficult to give.

That does not mean that research in itself is impossible to determine, but rather that each individual investor needs to determine for himself or herself which "research" pertains to the type of investment decisions he or she is evaluating. Besides asking my brother for his insight into video games, I also checked the total sales of video games per year in the United States on the Internet. I read several articles on the system that was being launched and its implications on the video game market. And I number crunched the stock in question with the formulas we've just learned in Lesson 12, "Evaluating Stocks," immediately after each of the company's previous new product launches.

Any investment decision you make should require some research. The extent is really up to you, but the time you are willing to contribute toward being ultrafamiliar with your investment decision correlates absolutely with the investment's success. By cheating on investment research time, you are ultimately cheating yourself. Make no mistakes about it; this kind of cheating *will* cost you cold hard cash.

BUY AND HOLD

Read this section twice. Buy and hold is a wonderful strategy for any newcomer to the market and is equally attractive to investors of any experience level. Basically, buy and hold works like this: Since the inception of stock markets, the value of the stocks being traded has eventually risen almost without exception. This passive strategy, *buy and hold,* works on the principle that if you purchase a stock and let it sit where it is long enough, you will eventually realize a profit. Whether that means 5, 10, or 20 years is uncertain, but remembering that your investments are part of a larger goal, it's pretty certain you'll see a profit before your dream becomes accessible and you are therefore ready to sell your shares.

PLAIN ENGLISH

Buy and hold is an investment strategy whereby an investor purchases a stock and leaves it alone. Buy and hold usually implies that dividends will be reinvested in subsequent purchases of the stock.

For a buy and hold strategy, you would want to consider stock in companies that have the potential to be around for the long term. Consider blue chip stocks or stocks with good growth potential to achieve this. In addition, instead of collecting dividends, newer investors should seriously consider reinvesting their dividends into subsequent stock purchases. Many companies will execute these subsequent purchases without adding sales loads, making the investment even better. In addition, by negating broker fees and allowing compound interest to perform its magic on the initial investment and its subsequent dividend reinvestments, even the most novice investor is better placed to realize a profit.

Finally, the most important benefit of the buy and hold strategy is almost certainly not having to spend an inordinate amount of time researching and following other investments. The buy and hold strategy is often referred to as the *buy and forget it* strategy for that very reason. As a new investor, you will have your hands full becoming familiar with the entirety of the market. Rather than make several different investments over time, you are bound to do better by thoroughly researching one investment and "letting it ride." Your broker will hate you because his or her commission is based on the number of total trades you perform, but your banker is going to love you as you keep those brokerage fees in your own account in the bank.

TIP

The magic of **compound interest** works on the principle that your subsequent profits are reinvested to later increase the amount of your interest. It's a circular phenomenon, but it really works as demonstrated in the table.

$10,000 Investment Growth Utilizing Compound Interest

Interest Rate	5 Years	10 Years	15 years	20 Years	25 Years
5%	$12,763	$16,289	$20,790	$26,533	$33,864
8%	$14,693	$21,589	$31,722	$46,610	$68,485
10%	$16,105	$25,937	$41,772	$96,463	$170,000
12%	$17,623	$31,058	$54,736	$96,463	$170,000
14%	$19,254	$37,379	$71,379	$137,435	$263,619

DOLLAR COST AVERAGING

Dollar cost averaging is another wonderful investment strategy that merits serious consideration by newer investors. In *dollar cost averaging,* you invest a specific amount at a regular interval: taking a set amount out of each paycheck, for example. The critics are undecided whether this type of investing produces an optimal or a mixed result, and statistics can be found to accommodate either view. What is certain, however, is that dollar cost averaging does not produce bad results, and it brings people to the table who might not otherwise be investing.

PLAIN ENGLISH

Dollar cost averaging is an investment strategy whereby an investor systematically invests a predetermined amount on a regular basis.

One of the single biggest excuses people give for not being in the stock market is that they don't have enough extra money to invest. However, if the average investor waited until he or she had hundreds of thousands of dollars to invest before becoming active, the American stock market would be a very different place than it is. People with large portfolios are rarely those who have received a lump sum equal to the current size of their portfolios. Rather, these large portfolios were created by making systematic smaller investments.

Regardless of the potential for optimal return with this strategy, the primary benefit of dollar cost averaging is to get people to invest relatively small amounts, which are intended to add up to a larger amount. Again, this strategy really works. The example of the $10,000 goal used in Lesson 11, "How to Pick Stocks," was not the result of a $10,000 initial investment, but rather the accumulation of systematic investing over a year's time.

By the way, dollar cost averaging is not guaranteed to produce higher stock prices for people who choose to invest this way. Should you be concerned about the price you will pay for stock as it fluctuates over the period of a year, you can use the following table to chart the average price you would have paid for a stock by using dollar cost averaging versus the average price of the stock over the same period. Used in retrospect (over the previous year), you can garner a pretty good idea of the potential for an optimal price using dollar cost averaging to purchase your prospective stock.

Month	Price per Share	Number of Shares Investment Would Purchase
January		
February		
March		
April		
May		
June		
July		
August		
September		
October		
November		
December		

To make the comparison, begin by finding the market price of the stock on the same day each month (say the first) of the previous year and listing it in the second column. Then determine how many shares your regular investment would have purchased each month and write that number in the third column. Next take the total number of shares you would own at the end of the year, add them together, and divide by 12. Do exactly the same with the price of shares, and compare how much the price you paid for each share differs from the average price of the share over the same period. You'll be surprised.

CONSTANT DOLLAR AVERAGING

Frankly, I'm not a big fan of constant dollar averaging. It's just too much work, not to mention too complicated math-wise. But, in the spirit of fairness, you, the investor, should be made aware of it so that you can decide whether it is appropriate for your own needs.

Using *constant dollar averaging,* an investor buys a set number of shares of stock, and adds to and subtracts from the amount invested in that stock to keep the amount of stock constant. As the price declines, the investor adds to the investment; as the price of the stock increases, the investor withdraws excessive cash.

PLAIN ENGLISH

Constant dollar averaging is an investment strategy whereby the investor adds or subtracts cash as necessary to keep the number of original stock purchased constant.

Success using the constant dollar averaging strategy is based on the assumption that as the value of your investment increases, you (the investor) collect its proceeds. This makes constant dollar averaging particularly attractive to investors who are looking for income from their stocks. As a novice investor, however, you will be charged with the responsibility of determining on a regular basis the fractions of cash and stock that will keep the stock level constant. In addition, by withdrawing the proceeds of your investment, you will deprive yourself of the power of compound interest. I'm not even going to mention the broker fees involved, but suffice it to say they are substantial and require serious consideration in this type of investment strategy.

For those reasons, while I'm not against constant dollar averaging, I just can't find a use for it in my own portfolio or in that of the novice investor.

The 30-Second Recap

- Determining your investment strategy, or how you will select your stock, is rarely as simple as selecting a predetermined set of rules and formulas. Instead, it should be composed of portions of various plans which are most appropriate for your particular situation.

- Recommendations are an investment strategy by which investors select their stock based on the outlook of, or the rating given by other people who may be in a better position to evaluate the company and its stock.

- Research as an investment strategy implies that the investor makes his or her stock selection based on the information uncovered by any number of sources the investor may consider relevant.

- Buy and hold is an exceptional investment strategy whereby an investor purchases stock and lets that decision stand for an extended period of time. In addition, buy and hold usually implies that any profits made from the stock such as dividends will be reinvested in subsequent purchases of the stock.

- Dollar cost averaging is an investment strategy whereby a person systematically invests a predetermined amount on a regular basis. Through the regular purchases of stock dollar cost averaging, a newer investor or one with little money initially can amass a sizeable portfolio over time.

- Constant dollar averaging is an investment strategy whereby the investor adds or subtracts the amount of cash necessary from his stock portfolio to keep the original number of stock purchased from fluctuating. This strategy is particularly popular with investors looking for regular income from their investments.

LESSON 14

How to Check Your Investments

In this lesson you will learn to reevaluate your portfolio periodically using the information listed in the daily stock tables that time has provided.

CONGRATULATIONS!

By now you have made your investment, and you are therefore officially a member of the investment community. Your responsibilities as an investor are not over yet, however. Maintenance on your investment is carried out in two ways:

- Reevaluating your portfolio
- Checking your stock's performance

The next two sections will show you exactly how to carry out this maintenance.

REEVALUATING YOUR PORTFOLIO

Reevaluating your portfolio means periodically recalculating your investment selections. Use the ever-increasing amount of information about your stocks to ensure that your original investment decision is still applicable in spite of changes in the market, such as a downturn in the economy, or other circumstances, such as a change in your income and investable income.

PLAIN ENGLISH

Reevaluating your portfolio means double-checking your investments at regular intervals. The stock market changes substantially from day to day, so it is very possible that as time passes your investment may no longer be the optimal place to put your money.

Whichever system you used initially to select your stock, you should use it again to ensure that the results are consistent enough to maintain your faith in the investment. In addition, since you now have tangible information regarding your stock's performance, you might want to consider using different methods to evaluate it.

The danger for most novice investors when they reevaluate their portfolios is that they place far too much importance on minor setbacks and changes. Reevaluating your portfolio is more about looking for major loopholes that you overlooked initially or evaluating unforeseen changes that now make an originally good investment bad. It is not the time to take out everything you own and reinvest it in something different. Exercising restraint is very important to newer investors for two reasons:

1. New investors are more prone to "play" with their investments. Hollywood is probably responsible for most of the portrayals of Wall Street and the world of investing, and, as with anything else Hollywood portrays, its idea of the world of investment is substantially more exciting than the reality. As a result, newer investors are often under the mistaken impression that if they are not trading their stocks (buying and selling), they are not getting the optimal return for their investment. Regular trading does make for exciting movies, but in real life it usually leads to a pretty dismal portfolio beset by broker fees.

TIP

> Put another way, reevaluating your portfolio is about reaffirming that your original decision is still the correct one, not about trying to pick that decision apart.

2. By trading stocks as opposed to letting them sit, investors are not allowing their stock to perform to its fullest potential. Remember that the greatest ally you have in the stock market is time. The stock market is geared toward investors who buy stock and keep it, rather than those who trade it frequently.

   Unlike the Las Vegas roulette wheel, capital gains and stock dividends tend to be highest among those that "let it ride"— even, or especially, when the stock has taken a downturn. The time when your stock has suffered a loss is not the time to sell it (unless of course, you firmly believe it will continue to go down until the company goes out of business). By selling your stock then, you will suffer an investment loss. However, if you let your investment sit, odds are heavily in favor of the stock, again with time, recovering that loss and even making a profit. Don't be faint-hearted … let it ride.

Remember, successful investing is not so much about buying and selling on a regular basis as it is about making educated investment decisions in the first place so that reaffirming your decisions later is not so difficult to do.

CHECKING YOUR STOCK'S PERFORMANCE

Once you have actually invested in a particular stock, you are no longer dealing with abstract ideas and numbers. Instead, you are dealing with cold hard cash. And, since this cash is yours, it's definitely important. Checking your stock's performance is every bit as essential as reevaluating your portfolio. In fact, the tangible information used to reevaluate your portfolio is gained by checking your stock's performance.

TIP

> Check your stock's performance with tools such as indices and financial media to determine whether your stock's behavior is consistent with your initial expectations of the stock's potential.

What's more, it's fun! Investment maintenance can be fun? You better believe it! As a matter of fact, checking on your stock is one of the privileges of stock ownership. While all your friends and family are reading the comics in the newspaper, you can turn right to the financial pages and impress the pants off them. You can tell those same friends and family to buy a certain product or use a service because you have a vested interest in the company (being part owner and all). You can watch CNN financial news and have it mean something to you. You can do all these things and more because you are now part of that elite group who stands by the bar at parties and discusses their investments. You are an investor. Don't miss out on the perks.

There are a number of vehicles for checking your stock's performance. As with the various types of investment strategies described in the previous lesson, here, too, you have a smorgasbord of methods to choose from. You probably won't need to know all the various methods, but you should pick a couple with which you are most comfortable and use them to check your stock's performance on a regular basis.

Descriptions of several of the more popular methods follow for your perusal. As you begin to check your stock's progress on different vehicles, do not be surprised to discover that each vehicle will probably give you a slightly different view of the stock's performance. That is because these vehicles are designed to measure a certain aspect of your stock, not the entire stock. Some will be concerned with the percentage rise or fall of your stock's prices, whereas others will compare the stock with other similar stocks to draw conclusions. Your job is to put all of these views together and create a cohesive picture that best depicts the performance of your stock. The vehicles you use should be ones that you are satisfied with and that you fully understand.

For example, in high school, each teacher gave you a grade in each subject—an A in math, a B in English, and an A in science, for example. At the end of the year, all those grades were added up to obtain your grade point average, and that number was a much better indicator of the kind of overall student you were than the single grade you received for your performance in just one particular subject. Stock maintenance is no different. Assemble those different "grades" that each measurement vehicle assigns to your stock's ability to pay dividends, produce capital gains, and remain liquid, for example. Then, with all that information before you, evaluate your stock.

READING THE STOCK TABLES

The closest thing to a computer printing of numbers that are randomly generated yet appear to be compiled by humans is the stock tables listed in the pages of the newspaper. With their masses of numbers, acronyms, and fine print, these tables can look overwhelming to the uninitiated reader.

Here's the secret, though: You don't need to know very much about the stock tables to use them. You just have to know enough to find the information you are looking for. Think of them as a phone book for the nearest large city. First, the phone book lists the name of every single person who lives in that city and who wants to be included in the book. By the same token, the stock tables list the name of every stock (well, not every stock, but you get the idea) in that market. For each name listed in the phone book, there is a phone number and an address. Then the same kind of information is given for businesses. The stock tables also list information relevant to the stock. When you compile all that information, you get a whole book, or in the case of financial information at least a couple of pages.

You are not frightened by the phone book because you know that you don't need to know everything in it, just one or two lines, and you know how to find that information. The following explanations will enable you to do the exact same thing in the stock tables: how to dive right in and come up with information specific to your stock. The sample stock table contains the information considered standard in a stock table. This information is available from *The Wall Street Journal, The New York Times,* or your local newspaper in a virtually identical format.

STOCK NAME

Reading from the left in the table, go to the third column. These are the *stock names,* or the names of the companies whose stocks are listed. Remember, not every single stock is listed, but as a newer investor it is a pretty safe bet that your stock will be popular enough to be up there. Because of a lack of space, the tables take a lot of liberty with abbreviations and acronyms, and they ram words together, so you will have to be kind of creative when looking up your stock. Alaska Airlines, for example, is listed as AlaskaAir. That's not so hard, but American Airlines is listed under its parent company name of AMR. Like the phone book, the stock tables do assume that you know at least the name of the company whose stock you want to look up.

PLAIN ENGLISH

The **stock name** is listed in the stock tables of the daily newspaper. The name usually appears as an abbreviation or an acronym. Motorola for example, is noted as MOT, Federal Express is noted as FDX, and Hertz Rent A Car is noted as HRZ.

TIP

The stock symbol assigned to American Airlines was AMR. When management created a parent company for the airline, the new holding company was christened with the stock symbol as a name.

52 Week					Yld		Vol				Net
Hi	Lo	Stock	Sym	Div	%	PE	100s	Hi	Lo	Close	Chg
25 13/16	19 3/8	ABN Am ADR	ABN	1.23e	6.2	...	566	20	19 3/4	9 7/8	–1/8
25 3/4	19 3/16	ABN AM pfA									
25 1/2	18 7/8	ABN Am pfA									
s39	20 99/128	AMR	AMR	Stk	...	5	8278	33 9/16	31 7/8	31 15/16	–1 3/16
61	35 1/2	AT&T	T	.88	2.5	19	181179	36 9/16	35 1/2	35 3/4	–1 3/16
36	27 11/16	AT&T Wrls	AWE				64745	27 13/16	26 1/2	26 1/2	–1 1/4
48 15/16	29 3/8	AbbotLab	ABT	.76f	1.8	26	54513	41 7/8	40 1/8	41 3/8	+13/16
s49 11/16	8 7/8	Abercrombie A	ANF		...	6	15195	9 1/4	8 7/8	8 7/8	–1/4
102	74 1/2	Agilent1Tch w			...	...	66	74 1/2	66 7/8	66 7/8	–7 5/8
46 3/8	23	AirProduct	APD	.76f	2.1	25	7482	36 5/16	34 11/16	36	+1
12 3/8	8 3/16	AlamaoGp	ALG	.24	1.9	17	97	12 1/2	12	12 3/8	+1/8
46 5/8	25 1/4	AlaskaAir	ALK		...	7	1019	29	28 5/8	28 5/8	–7/16

Next, notice that AMR is followed by Abercrombie (Abercrombie and Fitch) further down the page. This is because the stocks are listed in alphabetical order by the correct name of the company, not alphabetically by the strange shorthand for names. Since AMR is an acronym, (it's not really, read the preceding sidebar) it would precede a complete word. AT&T, which is a little further down the list, is also listed as an acronym rather than as American Telephone and Telegraph and therefore also precedes Abercrombie and Fitch.

You must also be aware that sometimes because of the way a corporation is structured, more than one listing will appear and the listings can be almost identical. In the example, AT&T is followed by AT&T Wrls, which stands for AT&T Wireless, an independent company. So, pay close attention.

And finally, if you look at the listing for ABN Am, you will notice that the name appears twice and the names are, in fact, identical. Notice, however, that each of the two listings is followed by "pfA" or "pfB," respectively. ABN Am (ABN Amro) is one company, but it is listed twice to display the information for both class A and class B of its preferred stock. (Do you remember the various classes of preferred stock from Lesson 5, "The Five Types of Stock"?) A "wt" could also follow, in which case the information would not be about the stock but rather about its warrants.

With all this information to think about, the first time you look up a particular stock, you may have to scan a moment or two to find it. This bit of searching is good, since it gives you the opportunity to become more familiar with the listings. Once you know what your stock listing looks like, you can aim right for it.

STOCK SYMBOLS

In the fourth column from the left is the *stock symbol*. This is the identifier that was initially used on ticker tapes and is still used today. The stock symbol is assigned to each stock by the market in which it is trading. It consists of a combination of one to four capital letters, depending on the market. The New York Stock Exchange and the American Stock Exchange both use one to three letters, for example, while the NASDAQ uses four.

PLAIN ENGLISH

> Depending on the market where stocks trade, **stock symbols** are composed of letter combinations of one to four letters. The NYSE can use one letter (Y for Algheny) to three (BDK for Black & Decker) while shares available through NASDAQ use up to four letters (Intel is known as INTC).

Often, electronic media will use the stock's symbol rather than its name to look up quotes. In addition, the stock symbol serves as a backup identifier for your stock in cases where several names or other information might confuse you.

Think of the stock symbol as an airport code. When you fly to Chicago, for example, your luggage tags read ORD for O'Hare Airport. If you're not flying to Chicago, you probably wouldn't make the effort to learn that particular code, but if you are going there, you should know O'Hare's code. The same applies to stock codes. Don't attempt to memorize every one, just the ones you have purchased, are considering for purchase, or in which you otherwise have an interest.

TIP

> The stock symbol is used so frequently in the financial world that it is a good idea to memorize the symbol for your stock.

HIGH-LOW

In the preceding table, the first column on the far left and the second column from the left show the stock's highest and lowest points, respectively, over the previous year. These are listed in dollars and cents. You will notice that most of the numbers are followed by fractions in denominations of 16. The fractions represent cents ($^{16}/_{16}$ = 100 cents, or $1), and the various equivalencies are given in the following table:

Fraction	Value in Cents
$^1/_{16}$	6¼
$^2/_{16}$	12½
$^3/_{16}$	18¼
$^4/_{16}$	25
$^8/_{16}$	50
$^9/_{16}$	56¼
$^{10}/_{16}$	62½
$^{11}/_{16}$	68¾
$^{12}/_{16}$	75
$^{13}/_{16}$	81¼
$^{14}/_{16}$	87½
$^{15}/_{16}$	93¾
$^{16}/_{16}$	100

PLAIN ENGLISH

The 52-week **high-low** comprises two separate entries in the daily stock table, one that lists the highest point and the other the lowest point (respectively) at which the stock was trading during the course of the past year.

Although the high-low information represents dollars and cents, you might want to consider changing the dollars and cents into percentages to better portray the volatility of the stock. This is easily done by determining the dollar amount of the change.

Let's use Abercrombie and Fitch as an example. The highest level the stock rose to over the last 52 weeks was 49¹¹/₁₆. The lowest the stock declined to was 8⅞. You would subtract the low, 8⅞, from the high, 49¹¹/₁₆, and get 41³/₁₆, or 41.18. Divide this number by the 52-week high (in this case 49¹¹/₁₆, or 49.68), and you will get the change in stock price in percentages. In this example, you would discover that the price of Abercrombie and Fitch varied a total of 82 percent over the last 52 weeks. That's a really volatile price.

Well it would be, but there's a catch. Do you see the little "s" before the first column? This is a *qualifier* that tells the reader that the stock split sometime in the last 52 weeks. A *stock split* is nothing more than a company recounting the number of shares of stock it has issued on the market, and dividing the number by (usually) half or reissuing two shares as three.

For example, if you owned one share of Abercrombie and Fitch, and it was worth $49, after the split you would own two shares, each worth $24.50. Or, in the case of a two to three split if you owned two shares at $49 each you would now own three shares worth $32.66 each. Companies make stock splits for many reasons, one of the largest being to keep the price of their stock low enough to attract investors.

Under normal circumstances, you would need to do a little more research to discover how the stock had been split, but for our example we will assume it was by half. This would change our high to 24.84 (49.68 ÷ 2) and the stock's real volatility to 35 percent. That's a lot easier to believe.

PLAIN ENGLISH

Qualifiers include symbols and initials in the stock tables that demonstrate under which circumstances the corresponding stock information should be considered. They are explained in detail in the stock key.

Other qualifiers run next to the 52-week highs and lows, and their presence can make a substantial difference in how the information is read. For example, when the stock has reached a price that is either higher or lower than anything in the past 52 weeks, it is designated as a new high or low with a small arrow pointing in the appropriate direction (up or down). When the stock is new, having been introduced within the last 52 weeks, it will be designated with a small "n" next to the first column. When looking up your stock, it is important to know what every symbol means. Fortunately, virtually all newspapers that run stock tables also run keys on how to read them. (Of course, you could always use this book, too!)

DIVIDENDS PER SHARE

The column to the right of the stock symbol, *Dividends per Share,* lists the anticipated annual dividends for the year. This figure is given in the same dollars and cents format as used in the High and Low listings. Although dividends are usually paid quarterly, all four payments have been combined here to give the annual payment.

PLAIN ENGLISH

Based on the amount of the last dividend paid, the entry in the **Dividends per Share** column provides an estimate of the anticipated dividend payments for a full year.

Most stock dividends are paid quarterly (once every three months), but this is neither a rule nor always true. Some companies pay dividends twice or thrice a year, and some not at all. This is another example of the type of information you will need to know before you can fully utilize the information in the stock tables.

It is also important to note that the dividend figure is not an actual figure, but an *anticipated dividend payment* based on the last quarter or regular declaration. "Anticipated" means that the number in the

Dividend per Share column is what the company thinks it is going to pay out over the next year. As with the projected P/E ratio discussed in Lesson 12, "Evaluating Stocks," the company uses the amount of the last dividend payment as a guideline to keep things reasonable. That way, a company can't project that it will pay $10 in dividends next quarter if last quarter it paid only $1.

Using the preceding information, we can look at AT&T's listing on our example. The Dividend per Share column lists .88 as the projected dividend payment for the year. For the purposes of our example, we will assume we know that AT&T pays its dividends quarterly (they do in real life, too, by the way). By dividing .88 by the four dividend payments (the one that has already happened and the three that are still outstanding for the year), it is safe to assume that AT&T paid out about .22 per share in dividends last quarter and presumes it will do the same in the next three projected quarters. It's true that the dividend payments could have been projected as 22 + 20 + 22 + 24; however, this particular measurement of a stock's dividend health assumes that the issue of importance is the *total* annual dividend payment.

Notice in the example that the space in the Dividend per Share column is blank next to Abercrombie and Fitch. That is because not all stocks pay dividends. It would be a pretty safe bet in this example to assume that Abercrombie and Fitch is a growth-oriented company that is reinvesting all its profits back into the company rather than paying them out to shareholders. That makes Abercrombie and Fitch stock a growth stock.

YIELD PERCENT

The column to the right of the Dividends per Share column is the *Yield Percent* (or Per Cent Yield) column. The figure within this column indicates the stock's value in relation to its current price and annual dividends—or the percentage of return based on the stock's closing price. The Yield Percent is calculated by dividing the dividend amount in the Dividends per Share column by the amount in the Close column (second column from the right).

The **Yield Percent** provides the ratio of dividends paid by a stock to its closing price. With this figure, investors can calculate the amount of income generated by the stock relevant to its initial investment requirement.

Please notice that the information in the Yield Percent column could be easily calculated by using information contained elsewhere in the table. The fact that a table, which is already so crowded, should make room for the calculation of an equation for its users is an indication of both the importance and the popularity of the Yield Percent figure. The information contained in this figure differs from the Current/Dividend Yield discussed in Lesson 12 primarily in its usage. As a result of the stock being actively in play from the investor's perspective, this figure provides not only a more current and fluid view of the stock's value, but the opportunity to distinguish and spot trends and evaluate the stock's performance as well.

While a stock's Current/Dividend Yield is but one figure, changes in the performance of the Yield Percent provide daily figures that can be charted or compared at regular intervals. This information can then be used against the initial amount projected by the company for the year's dividends. That information can enable the investor to adjust future projections by the company to calculate a more reasonable, and often a more accurate, projection.

Always compare how well the stock really did with what the issuing company said it would do. If the company continually aims high and falls short, future quotes are probably inflated. Should the company's quotes continually prove overly conservative, you would also adjust accordingly.

It is important to reemphasize that the Yield Percent is dependent on the decisions of the management of the stock's issuing company. The company can choose to pay dividends at whatever amount it sees fit. Or, the company can choose not to pay dividends at all. The absence of dividends would be indicated by an ellipsis (…), as noted next to AT&T Wrls in the example.

The Yield Percent listing's popularity is also due in large part to its easy-to-understand portrayal of the stock as a business. Again, this differs from the Current/Dividend Yield in that instead of having one figure, time provides a number of daily figures illustrating the stock's performance over time figures.

To illustrate, imagine buying a business such as a clothing shop. The Current/Dividend Yield figure would represent the price that you, the investor, paid for the business (stock), while the Yield Percent would represent the amount of money (dividends) made by the shop after changing hands. Like a clothing store owner, a stock owner also questions the rate of return on his or her investments. The Yield Percent provides a one-figure answer.

As with anything so easy, there is a catch. That one-figure answer is totally dependent on the company's decision on what, if any, portion of its earnings will be paid out to its investors. The Yield Percent is therefore not as much an indicator of how the company is doing as it is an indicator of how the company is being managed—the portrayal of the company that its management wants you, the investor, to see.

P.E. Ratio

To the right of the Yield Percent column is the *Price/Earnings ratio,* or *P.E. ratio.* Even though the name is the same as the Price Earnings ratios (Trailing, Standard, and Forward) discussed in Lesson 12, the figure listed here is not calculated using the stock's dividend payments. Instead, by dividing the P.E. ratio into the stock's current price, the investor can discover the stock's dollar earnings per share.

PLAIN ENGLISH

The **P.E. ratio** in the stock tables is calculated by dividing the issuing company's total earnings by the number of outstanding shares. This way, investors can analyze the actual money generated by their investment without the confusing factors associated with dividend payments.

The P.E. ratio is useful in that it doesn't portray the value of the stock as compared to its selling price but rather as compared to how much the stock is earning. Or, in other words, the price of one share of stock as compared to the earnings of the company.

Think of it this way: Using the same clothing store example, let's assume that three different clothing stores exist in town. One clothing store owner pays all profits to his or her investors, the second reinvests all profits back into the business, and the third reinvests some of the profits back into the store and pays some out to the investors. To make things more confusing, each store has a different number of investors. It would be difficult to determine which store was actually doing the best business simply by using only their dividend payments.

However, if we could determine the total amount each store had made in profits, we could then divide this number by the number of investors. The resulting figure would provide a much clearer view of the amount of return each store was generating on each dollar invested, regardless of where those returns were going or how many people were involved.

Similarly, investors use the P.E. ratio to determine the relative value, or what kind of return their investment provides. This is often referred to as "trading at X times the company's earnings," or simply "X times earnings." For example, in the sample stock table, notice that Abbot-Lab's P.E. ratio is 26 times earnings. This means that the current price of AbbotLab's stock, $41.38, is 26 times more than the company's earnings per share of $1.59 for the last year. Or, in other words, if Abbot Labs continued to earn the same amount of profits each year and the company never changed (an absolute impossibility), in 26 years its stock would pay for itself.

Stocks trading at more than 20 times earnings are considered to have "high" P.E. ratios, and stocks trading at less than 10 times earnings are considered to have "low" P.E. ratios. More important, the same warning given earlier about rules being quickly dismissed in the realities of stock trading also applies to P.E. ratios. Remember that the P.E. ratio of a stock is useful only when it is used within the total context of the stock, including such factors as industry, past performance, and current market conditions.

VOL 100s

The figure in the column to the right of the P.E. Ratio column is the *Vol 100s* listing, and it contains the number of shares of the stock that traded on that particular day. This number is rounded off to the nearest thousand, so two additional zeros need to be added to the listed figure.

PLAIN ENGLISH

> The **Vol 100s** listing contains the number of total shares of each stock that changed hands during the trading day. When the figure in this column is under 10,000, it must be multiplied by 100 to obtain the correct number of traded shares.

Many people explain this figure as representing the number of round lots of shares that have been sold. However, not all stocks sell in lots of 100, so this explanation is not consistent with the listed figures. I use the explanation that there simply isn't enough room to list the entire number and that the most insignificant digits of the figure are truncated—the figure is rounded off to fit.

Either way, what is certain is that the volume of shares being traded is a good indicator of whether a stock is being actively traded or virtually ignored. The other measurements have concerned themselves predominantly with the condition of the stock and its issuing company. The volume of stock traded, however, measures the supply and demand of the stock in the market. This information can be interpreted any number of ways, depending on the circumstances. However, when a stock is trading at unusually high levels, the high volume is often an indication of extreme volatility in either the price of the individual stock or the market as a whole.

To determine whether the number of shares actually traded that day represents a substantial portion, you would first need to know the total number of shares the company has issued. Obviously, what is considered substantial is arbitrary. Each investor would have a different idea of what constitutes substantial. The markets, rather than attempting to determine this, present the information and let the investors decide for themselves. They do, however, note the most actively traded stocks (the top 40 for the NYSE and the largest 20 for the AMEX) as a percentage of their average trading volumes. These are underlined for easy spotting.

This is not usually presented to indicate the preference of any market, but because stocks being heavily traded are usually reacting to a recent event or announcement that has changed the company's status quo. Stocks may be selling quite heavily in response to an interest rate hike, or they may be bought up in response to an analyst's prediction or rating. Whatever the reason, the stock's circumstances are changing, and the volume of shares traded will reflect the response to that change by the market as a whole.

High-Low

The next two columns to the right of the Vol 100s column list the highest price and the lowest price, respectively, that the stock reached during the trading day. Like the Vol 100s figure, the numbers in these columns do not measure any aspect of the stock from an internal point of view but rather measure how the stock is perceived in the market.

PLAIN ENGLISH

The daily **high-low** entries list the highest and lowest points at which the stock was trading over the course of the day. Used together, you can use these figures to better understand the volatility of the stock. Remember that this is different from the high-low listing discussed earlier which shows the highest and lowest price of the stock over the last year.

During the stock trading day, investors will buy some stocks and sell others. As a very general rule, when more shares of the stock are being sold than purchased, the price of the stock will drop because of the laws of supply and demand. These same rules would cause the price of the stock to rise should more shares be purchased than sold. Interestingly enough, these peaks and valleys of the stock price create a self-fulfilling prophesy. As the stock crests at new heights and drops to new lows, these new levels will, in turn, cause investors to buy and sell the stock even more.

Although it is not possible to chart the entire trading day of each stock in these tables, the tables do provide the highest and lowest points the stock reached on its journey to the end of the day. Subtracting the lowest price of the day from the highest provides a figure known as the *spread*. The spread accurately measures the volatility of the price of the stock during the trading day. Like the volume of stock traded, the spread is completely dependent on the stock's perceived value in the market, rather than the value attributed to the stock by its issuing company. Perceived values will be what drives sales and purchases of the stock.

CAUTION

Since the perception of a stock's value is heavily influenced by events and announcements in the market, the spread is more of an indicator of the market's reaction to these events, rather than the condition of the company.

The perceived value can be thought of as the ultimate in self-fulfilling prophecies. A company that maintains a low perceived value could, in theory, eventually lose all its investors and go out of business as a result of this perception, regardless of the actual financial condition of the company. Perhaps it is more a case of what came first—the bad perception or the subsequent bad financial health of the company that confirms the perception.

CLOSE

The figure in the second column from the right is, hands down, the easiest of all the information in the table to read. No knowledge of abbreviations, background research, or mathematical computations is required. The figure in this column is the *close,* the price of the stock at the end of the closing day. The ease of understanding this figure is not, however, a reflection of its importance.

> **PLAIN ENGLISH**
>
> The **close** is the stock's current price or the price at which the stock settled at the end of the trading day.

The closing price of the stock can be compared, for example, with the original price at which the stock was purchased in order to show any gains or losses from the original amount invested. Without requiring the use of mathematical equations, this method provides a very basic and completely accurate picture of an investment's performance.

The closing price can also be compared to the high and low prices in the previous two columns to discover where in the volatility of the trading day the price of the stock eventually settled. Using the AT&T Wrls stock in our sample stock table, for example, we can determine that the stock got as high as $27^{13}/_{16}$ before bottoming out at $26\frac{1}{2}$. Unfortunately, in our example, that's also the price at which the stock closed for the day. Finally, remember that many of the equations used earlier require the use the stock's closing price.

Investors can crunch numbers relevant to this or compared to that in order to come up with a dizzying volume of statistical data that will reveal any aspect of a stock's performance or support any view. At the end of the day, however, the simple way to determine the success of any investment is simply to ask, "Is it more valuable now than when I first bought it?" Without any flourishes, the closing price of the stock will announce just that.

NET CHANGE

The figure in the last column on the right shows the *net change,* the change in the closing price of the stock from the previous day's closing price. Comparing this information with the current day's closing price gives the most basic indicator of the behavior of the stock's price from day to day. In our sample table, we can see that the change in the price of AirProduct's stock from the previous day was +$1. Using the current day's closing price of 36, we can deduce that AirProduct's stock price yesterday at closing was $35 per share, or that the value of AirProduct's stock went up $1 today.

> **PLAIN ENGLISH**
>
> The **net change** is an indicator of the difference between the stock's current day closing price and the stock's previous day closing price.

In addition, however, remembering that the previous day's closing price is the same price at which the stock began the trading day, we can compare that price to the stock's current day high and low to get an even better picture of the stock's volatility during the day.

For example, in the sample stock table, we can determine that AgilentTch started the trading day at 74¹¹⁄₁₆. The stock closed at 66⅜, which is only ⅝, or .50, higher than the lowest point the stock hit that day. In this case, adding the net change loss to the closing price of

AgilentTch (66⅝ + 7⁵⁄₁₆), we can determine that it started the trading day at 73⁵⁄₁₆. The stock rose only a little higher during the trading day to its highest point of 74½, or a little more than half a point, and then plunged to 66⅝, which, as we have already determined, was very close to the lowest point the stock reached during the day. This information gives a clear picture that this was a really bad day for AgilentTch. Combined with the information in the rest of the table, we know that AgilentTch at some point within the last year was trading at $162 per share (in the 52-Week High column) and that it has also traded as low as 39¹³⁄₁₆. Although today's performance wasn't the worst one ever experienced by AgilentTch, it's still pretty bad.

TIP

> Please remember that the net change information by itself doesn't provide the whole picture. It is, however, a definite indicator that anyone interested in investing in this stock needs to learn what the relevant information is before deciding whether this stock is a good investment.

MISCELLANEOUS INFORMATION

In addition to the information discussed here and the keys to understanding the notations used, the stock pages of newspapers provide a vast array of other types of information regarding stocks and their markets. This type of *miscellaneous information* includes lists of ...

- Stocks that have reached new highs and lows.

- Stocks that are trading in odd lots.

- Stocks that are being offered for the first time (IPOs).

- Exchange rates of the U.S. dollar around the world, which could affect U.S. investments.

The stock pages will also contain expert analyses of stock performances, recommendations for stock picks and duds, and even articles discussing news events and their impact on stocks and the markets.

The amount and type of information varies from day to day as well as from newspaper to newspaper. It is a good idea to familiarize yourself with these areas and of course to also look up your own stock's performance. By doing so, you will be in a better position to discover information you might otherwise have missed that could affect your current holdings or affect your decisions regarding future investments. Eventually you will become increasingly familiar with the markets, their behavior, and your subsequent reactions to that behavior.

PLAIN ENGLISH

Miscellaneous information is a general term for any information contained in the financial pages in addition to the information contained in the stock tables. This information can include topics such as currency exchange rates, IPO offerings, and analyst predictions.

Even as you have overcome your initial discomfort with the stock tables by learning to interpret the information contained in the stock listings, you will do the same with the financial pages after repeated exposure. As a child, you probably read little more than the comic pages in the newspaper. By expanding your reading as you grew up to include the headlines, job listings, personals, and weekend magazine, you grew increasingly comfortable with the kind of information available there, even if you didn't necessarily need to know it all on a day-to-day basis. The true is same with the financial pages. Find out what it all means by reading everything a couple of times. After a while, you will learn which columnists or listings provide helpful information and you will always check them out.

Let's use what we have learned. Using our sample stock table, look up Alamo's stock. We would find it alphabetically under the name the

Alamo Group or AlamoGp on the table. We know that the stock symbol for the Alamo Group stock we bought is ALG, which we can double-check on the table to ensure we are looking at the right listing. We know that the Alamo Group's stock closed at 12⅜, up from yesterday's closing price of 12¼. We can determine that the price of the stock rose from 12¼ to 12½ and dropped to a low of $12 even before finally settling at the price of 12⅜. Finally, we can see that the current price is a new high for the Alamo Group over the last year. We can also see that Alamo expects to pay out 24 cents in dividends over the next year and that represents a very low yield compared to the stock price. This gives the stock a low yield for its price, 1.9 percent. We can also see that the stock is trading at 97 times earnings. We then apply this information to the standards and expectations that we have already determined are appropriate for our own investments to see whether this is a stock in which we might like to invest.

THE 30-SECOND RECAP

- Reevaluate your portfolio periodically to ensure that your original investment decision is still a good one in light of changes that may have since occurred in the market or in your financial objectives or circumstances.

- Stock names and corresponding stock symbols are listed in the daily stock tables of the newspaper.

- The highest and lowest prices a stock has attained over the last year are listed under 52 Weeks high-low, while the previous day's trading day is listed under high-low. The price at which the stock closed the previous day is listed under the Close column.

- Statistical information is available in the stock tables including the stock's price to earning ratio and the current yield, both of which are noted under headings of the same name.

LESSON 15

The Ticker Tape, Stock Indices, and Other Media

In this lesson you will learn about further sources of information on your stock's performance.

THE TICKER TAPE

No image better represents the United States stock markets than the *ticker tape*. The little one-inch-wide strip of paper is as synonymous with following the performance of stocks and their markets as it is with heroes' welcomes and parades. Ironically, you would be hard pressed to find an actual ticker tape machine outside of a museum or, for that matter, to find a parade that still uses the discarded strips. Computers have replaced ticker tape machines, and returning heroes are now showered in celebration with shredded paper and phone books.

PLAIN ENGLISH

Originally, the **ticker tape** referred to an actual machine. Today the term is used to describe an electronic ribbon that carries information on stock trades currently occurring in the market.

Today's ticker tape usage is a far cry from the machine's heyday, when between a quarter and a third of a mile of tape ran through the ticker on a daily basis, with the machine providing an endless stream of audible ticks as it reported on the activity in the United States stock markets. Considering the sheer volume of information that would have to pass through a ticker tape today to report on the markets, it is glaringly obvious why its usefulness is long past and why the ticker tape machine has become but a fond memory.

The information contained on the ticker tape, however, is still available in many places. Electronic ticker tapes run in such varied locations as the bottom of your television screen and oversize billboards in Times Square (on the corner of the Morgan Stanley building). There's even a McDonald's on Wall Street that runs an electronic ticker tape during the day, since the customers obviously have a vested interest.

The information on these ticker tapes isn't nearly as comprehensive as the information on the stock tables, and it runs past pretty quickly, so little opportunity exists to gather what information it has.

BP	FBC	AMXPB	ASP	TX	RUS	MX	UNP	C	GLW	PHH
6⅞	9¼	25S40½	5s21⅝	200,000s4	6⅛	4¾	6	6	6⅞	5⅜

THE TOP ROW

The information on the ticker tape is displayed in two rows. The top row contains information identifying the stock whose performance is being listed—the symbol of the stock, for example. Since insufficient room exists to list the full names of the stocks, investors must already know the stock symbol. Stock symbols here can run from one to four letters as appropriate for the corresponding market.

Of the 26 letters in the English alphabet, 22 are used individually to note stocks. The letters *I, O, Q,* and *W* are not used, because *I* and *O* look too much like the numerals 1 and 0. In addition, *Q* is reserved for companies that have filed bankruptcy. *W* isn't used because it is too easily confused with the lowercase letter *w* which, when it follows a stock symbol, denotes a warrant. Still, having a whole letter to yourself is pretty prestigious, so it goes without saying that the stocks assigned to those 22 letters are major companies. AT&T, for example, gets the letter *T,* and Sears gets the letter *S;* both are major old and respected companies.

The order of the listings is alphabetical by the actual name of the company, not by its stock symbol, so the symbols on the tape appear to be listed without rhyme or reason, unless you know the correct name of the company as well as its stock symbol.

TIP

> Know the names and/or symbols of a couple of stocks that precede your own so you won't miss your listing when it passes.

Following the stock symbol, you may discover the symbol "Pr." This indicates that the following information pertains to the stock's preferred classes. In the event that the company has issued more than one class of preferred stock, the appropriate class would be designated by following the Pr symbol with the letters *A, B, C,* and so forth.

You learned earlier that stocks are often traded on more than one market. As a result, when the location of the trade is relevant, the symbol may be followed by an ampersand (&) and another letter. The letter signifies the corresponding market where the trade took place, and its use indicates that the market itself is a relevant piece of information and needs to be considered when determining the performance of the stock. In our sample, we can see that a relevant ICN pharmaceuticals trade took place on the NASDAQ because of the ampersand and the notation of the letter *N.*

THE SECOND ROW

Once you have found the appropriate listing, look in the second row to discover the trading activity of the stock. When a price alone follows the stock symbol, it indicates that the trade being reported took place in the amount of 100 shares. Again, this is a throwback to the assumption that all shares trade in round lots, which we have established is not always true.

In addition, the listed price is not always accurate; it assumes that you as an investor already know the *range* within which the stock was trading. In the sample, note that British Petroleum is listed as trading 100 shares at the price of 6⅞. This is not accurate, because British Petroleum was actually trading at 46⅞. The ticker tape assumes that you as an investor in British Petroleum already knew its stock had been trading in the $40 to $50 range.

The ticker tape is not totally sadistic, however. In cases where the stock is trading in multiples of 100, this fact is indicated by preceding the number of 100-share multiples with a capital S. In the sample, for example, we can determine that the B class of American Express preferred stock just traded 2,500 shares at $40.50 per share. This rule holds true for up to 10,000 shares. Should any number greater than 10,000 precede the capital S, the number should not be multiplied by 100. This designation can be used to represent a block trade, or it might also be used to signify a share that is not trading in round lots of 100.

TIME DELAY

Finally, be aware that the information on the ticker tapes is always released to investment houses and brokers first. Only after a 15-minute delay is the information released to the general public at large. In addition, the introduction of the computerized quote machine now used by most brokers enables them to access greater amounts of information in real time, or virtually up to the second the trade is made. Although these innovations will further make the ticker tape obsolete, its future existence is nevertheless almost certainly guaranteed, not by what it is capable of providing but out of respect for the heights to which its past performance has brought the United States markets.

THE INDICES

Attempting to understand the movements of the market as a whole is a difficult if not an impossible task. However, understanding these movements, as well as the reasons for them, is fundamental to making projections for individual stocks and grasping their performances within the parameters of their circumstances. In other words, you've got to know how the stocks have done before you can guess how they will do. Furthermore, you've got to know the conditions of the playing field before you can decide whether their earlier efforts are any indication of future performance under the same or different circumstances.

Indices, as a result of their remarkable accuracy rate, are the most accepted measurement for information about a stock's health. As an investor, you are charged with checking the performance of your stock by assembling several indications of various aspects of your stock's health, thereby creating an overall financial health picture. This overall picture is very much like a grade point average or a financial market index. Here are the indices to consult:

- Dow Jones Average

- NASDAQ National Market System Composite Index

- Standard & Poor's 500

- AMEX Market Value Index

- NYSE Composite Index

- Russell Indices

- Wilshire 5000 Equity Index

PLAIN ENGLISH

The **indices** are indicators of value changes in representative stock groupings. An index is composed of a predetermined number of stocks whose prices are combined and averaged either on the number of figures or on an earlier established benchmark.

An *index* compiles the prices of representative stocks to obtain an overall average of the health of the market being indexed. Think of it this way: Let's say you are the principal of a small elementary school for grades one through six. You want to discover the effectiveness of the new teaching methods you have implemented in order to determine whether or not you will continue to invest money in these initiatives. You could give every student in the school a before and an after test and then compile and compare that data. The logistics and administration of the tests could quickly become horrific though, depending on the number of students. Also, you couldn't really compare the data from grade to grade, since each grade would require a different test to correspond to the varying levels of ability.

You could, however, give the test to a sample of five students per grade. This would reduce the amount of data to 30 tests (5 samples × 6 grades = 30). You could even add the different grade-level scores together to get an overall score. By comparing the results with the same figure derived from the before-test data, you as a principal could get an overall idea of how the teaching methods had affected the quality of instruction. The advantage of this method is that only one overall score is needed and the disruption to your school is minimal.

In much the same way, indices, using just one figure or score, give a broad overview of how current events are affecting the market. An index adds up the prices of a predetermined number of stocks that are considered to best represent their markets. The sum is then averaged to provide an overall figure that is intended to represent the market as a whole.

Using the same elementary school example, by increasing the amount of data—namely, increasing the number of students sampled—would also provide a more accurate average. This is because by expanding the sample, the average is less affected by the changes of individual stocks. The trick, then, is to determine how much information can be handled effectively without decreasing accuracy.

Indices can measure any type of market, and anyone can create an index. Indices measure exchanges such as the New York Stock Exchange as well as industries such as utilities. Indices can also measure collective groups, such as new companies with little or substantial capitalization. The trick is to pick the stocks that best represent the market being measured. In addition, to further ensure that they remain representative, indices must be capable of incorporating adjustments based on the effects of progress and changes. For that reason, indices are active, constantly being monitored for any necessary formulaic adjustments, including the replacement of the representative stocks.

TIP

Several of these indices have achieved phenomenal popularity. The Dow is used almost synonymously with the overall market. When we say the market rose 10 points or dropped 15, what we are actually referring to is the change in the Dow index.

The good news is you don't have to do a thing. All this mathematical stuff is performed by nameless, faceless people with no friends or family. All you have to do is take the final product: a one-number answer that lets you know how "everything" is doing. In addition, chances are that an index already exists to provide an overall grade for whatever group of stocks you consider a market. Financial newsletters and the Internet make literally thousands of indices available just for the taking. Think of the indices as movie critics. Each one wants to present his or her market indicator or film critique in the hopes that you will agree it is the best description of the entirety.

THE DOW JONES AVERAGE

The *Dow Jones Average* is the most highly accepted and regarded index in existence. Its inception more than 100 years ago in 1884 confirms its credential as the market's longest-running index. This index is more than simply prestigious; because of its unparalleled run, the Dow has amassed market data unequalled by any competing index. This data enables the Dow to continue to make further depictions with success rates much higher than those of the competition. For these reasons, the Dow's depiction of the state of the American markets is almost absolute.

PLAIN ENGLISH

> The most prestigious of all the indices, the **Dow Jones Average** is a series of four separate indices composed of stock currently trading on the New York Stock Exchange. It is considered to best represent the activity of the market and the U.S. economy.

Charles Dow, founder of *The Wall Street Journal,* created the Dow Jones Average in 1884. His initial list of 11 stocks has since grown to 65 companies subdivided into four categories as follows:

- **The Industrial Average** lists blue chip stocks of 30 companies in industries ranging from computer technology such as IBM, to raw steel manufacturers such as Bethlehem Steel.

- **The Utility Average** lists the stocks of 15 power-producing companies, such as Consolidated Edison (Con-Ed) for electricity, and Consolidated Natural Gas for gas.

- **The Transportation Average** lists stocks in 15 transportation-based companies ranging from airlines, such as TWA, to move-it-yourself truck rental companies, such as Ryder.

- **The Composite Average** lists the average of the combined 65 stocks listed by the other three averages.

The most commonly used of these averages is the Dow Jones Industrial Average. Remember, however, that this is but one portion of the whole Dow Jones average. These 30 stocks, all traded on the floor of the New York Stock Exchange, have been chosen by the editors of *The Wall Street Journal* because they are thought to accurately reflect the state of the American markets. Because of the sheer number of types of industries represented on the stock exchange, however, many critics believe that an index of 30 stocks cannot possibly depict the state of the American markets accurately.

In addition to industry representation issues, the stocks on the Industrial Average receive criticism for being exclusively blue chip stocks. Critics of the index believe this exclusivity also limits its ability to effectively represent the different responses of various types of stock to the same stimuli.

One of the methods employed by the Dow to nullify some of the extenuating market circumstances in its averages is the use of a *divisor*. In a proper average, the number of entrant figures is the same number as the one used to divide the total sum. In the case of the Dow and many other indices, however, this number has been adjusted to (hopefully) provide a more accurate average.

The divisors used to calculate the Dow Jones Average appear daily as a footnote to the Dow Jones Averages tables on the stock pages. The four averages used to compile the Dow are ...

The Industrial Average	.18238596
The Utility Average	1.8618942
The Transportation Average	.20890294
The Composite Average	1.0127139

Also included in the Dow Jones Averages tables is the position of the Dow during the last five business days as well as the last two years.

Anyone looking at the Dow today will find it rising and falling within the 10,000 to 11,000 range, and it is safe to assume that the average price of a stock listed on this index is nowhere in this range. This is because the Dow is not reporting in dollars and cents, but in points. These points constitute a scale that is used for measuring the market rather than actual prices.

Furthermore, as the world of trading evolves and expands, the Dow has found itself ill equipped to adjust for the influences of trading in other countries on American markets. In response, the Dow has created the *World Index,* a new measurement to account for the ramifications of global trading. This new index, in addition to attempting more-accurate worldwide reporting, demonstrates the Dow's willingness to make inherent changes to the infrastructure of its averages in order to incorporate new data and changing market conditions.

Despite its inherent flaws and criticisms, no index is more closely followed or has such an established position in the American marketplace than the Dow.

A stock's position on any of the Dow Averages is never assured. The editors of *The Wall Street Journal* change the stocks periodically to ensure that the selected stocks still best represent their corresponding markets. The stocks listed in each average appear regularly in the financial pages. Currently, the 30 stocks listed on the Industrial Average are the following:

- AT&T
- Alcoa
- American Express
- Boeing
- Caterpillar
- Citigroup
- Coca-Cola
- Disney
- DuPont
- Eastman Kodak
- ExxonMobil
- General Electric
- General Motors
- Hewlett-Packard
- Home Depot
- Honeywell
- Intel
- IBM
- International Paper
- Johnson & Johnson
- McDonald's
- Merck
- Microsoft
- Minnesota Manufacturing and Mining
- J.P. Morgan
- Phillip Morris
- Proctor & Gamble
- SBC Communcations
- United Technologies
- Wal-Mart

THE NASDAQ NATIONAL MARKET SYSTEM COMPOSITE INDEX

If the Dow is the establishment, the *National Association of Securities Dealer Automated Quotations (NASDAQ) National Market System Composite Index* is the workhorse of market indices. This index monitors common stock that is traded on the NASDAQ system (also known as over-the-counter stocks).

PLAIN ENGLISH

The **NASDAQ National Market System Composite Index** is an index composed of over-the-counter stock that is being traded on the NASDAQ system. Owing to the type of stocks inherent in this market, it is considered to best represent younger, more mobile companies.

The index is compiled of stocks from the following six industries:

- Banking
- Finance
- General Industry
- Insurance
- Transportation
- Utilities

These industries are deemed to best represent the overall health of the American markets. However, because of the primary types of stocks listed on the NASDAQ, this index is considered to better represent more-speculative stocks, including startup companies in the preceding six industries.

This same qualifier, however, is also used as the reason why the NASDAQ best represents the market as a whole. The reasoning here is that smaller, less-established companies are quicker to feel the reverberations in the market. In addition, the sheer number of stocks listed on the NASDAQ (over 31,000) gives it the highest proportion of American stocks represented.

Note that although both indices are attempting to accurately represent the health of the American market, the Dow is composed of stocks that trade on the New York Stock Exchange and the NASDAQ lists stocks that trade over the counter. As a result, it quickly becomes obvious that these two indicators may not necessarily react similarly to the day's events. Differences in the mix of types and numbers of securities as well as the divisors used to compute the averages further widen these differences. In all fairness, the different indices generally behave similarly. However, the growing effects of international trading and the increasing volatility of many of today's markets, such as computer technology, have continually proved that the results of these different indices are not necessarily interchangeable, even when attempting to measuring the same markets.

THE STANDARD & POOR'S 500

Standard & Poor's Corporation, a subsidiary of McGraw-Hill, Inc., is a well-respected financial company, providing a variety of services such as stock and bond ratings and publication of a number of financial advisory reports. In 1957 Standard & Poor's launched its own index, the *Standard & Poor's 500,* or the S&P 500 as it is more commonly known.

PLAIN ENGLISH

The **Standard and Poor's 500** is an index composed of the 500 largest stocks trading on the NYSE and the NASDAQ. The 500 stocks are further subdivided into four industry indices that are meant to measure the results of these particular industries.

Like the Dow and the NASDAQ, a significant portion of the S&P 500's popularity is a result of the high regard with which investors hold its issuing company. More important, however, is the continuing accuracy of the index. The S&P is particularly well suited for this, as it is composed of the 500 largest stocks that trade on either the New York Stock Exchange or the NASDAQ system. This prevents the S&P 500 from being unduly affected by the movements of one particular market. In addition, with a sample base of 500, this index is also less affected by extreme circumstances surrounding any one particular stock. Finally, to compensate for the varying sizes of the 500 stocks, each stock is weighted within the divisor formula to adjust for its own particular size within the context of the index as a whole.

But the safeguards as well as the similarities don't stop there. The stocks listed on the S&P 500 are further broken down into four industry segments that are designed to represent the overall health of the American markets. Also, in a further attempt to adjust for the appropriate level of effect that each industry has on the market as a whole, the number of stocks assigned to each industry is not equal. These four industrial segments and the corresponding number of stocks assigned to them in the S&P 500 are listed in the following table:

Industry	Number of Represented Stocks
General Industry	400
Finance	40
Transportation	20
Utilities	40

Like the four Dow averages, each of the four S&P 500 segments has its own individual index, although the total of the four is used substantially more often than the individual averages.

Because of these stringent safeguards in selecting the samples that compose the index, the S&P 500 has become particularly popular with people who are directly or indirectly involved in finance. Investment managers, for example, as well as technical analysts, banks, and insurance companies, all rely heavily on the S&P 500 as an indication of the market's health. As a result, the S&P is often used to index portfolios. This means that the stocks selected for inclusion in the S&P 500 are also selected to create individual or institution portfolios. Creating your own personal portfolio to match the S&P would, in theory, position the portfolio to mirror the success, or failure, of the S&P 500 directly.

THE AMEX MARKET VALUE INDEX

The *American Stock Exchange (AMEX) Market Value Index,* or the AMEX index as it is more popularly known, lists 800 stocks that trade on the American Stock Exchange. Much like the NASDAQ, then, the AMEX index is primarily concerned with the performance of stocks in that particular market, rather than being geared to represent the overall American markets as a whole.

PLAIN ENGLISH

The **AMEX Market Value Index** is composed of 800 stocks trading on the American Stock Exchange. This type of index believes the health of the American economy is best represented by the performance of the proprietary market.

THE NYSE COMPOSITE INDEX

Similarly to the Dow and the S&P 500, the *New York Stock Exchange (NYSE) Composite Index* is composed exclusively of stocks that trade on the floor of the New York Stock Exchange. The NYSE Composite Index is composed of all of the stocks on the NYSE, over 1,600 in all.

PLAIN ENGLISH

Like the AMEX index, the **New York Stock Exchange Composite Index** is primarily concerned with portraying the activities of its own exchange. The New York Stock Exchange Composite Index is composed of all stocks that trade at the NYSE, some 1,600 stocks in total.

Also unlike the other indices, the NYSE Composite is not quoted in representational points, but rather in the actual dollars and cents that have been calculated to actually represent the average price of all stocks in the New York Stock Exchange. Although this method does not provide an accurate representation of any individual stock listed on the index, it does provide an easy-to-use indicator of the health of the NYSE, and subsequently the American market as a whole.

THE RUSSELL INDICES

As you may have already noticed, the number of stocks sampled varies from index to index. Nevertheless, it is a generally accepted rule that the larger the sample, the more accurate the subsequent measure will prove to be. The Frank Russell Company utilizes this theory in compiling the *Russell Indices,* three indices that measure the movement of companies with varying levels of capitalization. The three are the Russell 3000, the Russell 2000, and the Russell 1000.

PLAIN ENGLISH

The **Russell Indices** are three indices used to rate the activities of stocks based on their market capitalization. The smallest, the Russell 1000, measures the activities of the 1,000 largest capitalized companies, whereas the more famous Russell 2000 measures the remaining capitalized companies.

To create these indices, the Frank Russell Company compiles the stock prices of the largest 3,000 companies based on *market capitalization*—the value of a company based on the market price of its total outstanding stock. Together, these form the Russell 3000. More widely used, however, are the other two: the Frank Russell 1000, which is composed of the biggest 1,000 of the initial 3,000; and the Frank Russell 2000, which is composed of the balance.

TIP

> **Market capitalization** is determined by multiplying the market price of one share by the total number of outstanding shares. In this way, the value of all outstanding stock, or the market capitalization of the company, is discovered.

The Russell 2000, which is also known as the Russell 2000 Small Stock Index, is widely regarded as the best measure of the stock performance of smaller companies with capitalization ranging from $25 million to $275 million. This index is particularly important, because smaller companies are considered to react more quickly and therefore provide a better indication of pending market changes. This knowledge can enable an investor to spot trends faster and thus adjust his or her portfolio accordingly to best handle the looming circumstances.

THE WILSHIRE 5000 EQUITY INDEX

The *Wilshire 5000* is the granddaddy of them all. It is composed of the prices of all stocks traded on the New York Stock Exchange, the American Stock Exchange, and the NASDAQ system for which there is a quote. This astounding number, more than 5,000 in all, confirms the Wilshire 5000's position as the largest of the popular indices. The value of the stocks listed is easily billions of dollars, ensuring that the Wilshire 5000 is affected minimally by extenuating extreme circumstances surrounding either a particular stock or an individual market.

PLAIN ENGLISH

> The **Wilshire 5000 Index,** the largest of the popular indices, is composed of all quoted stocks on the NYSE, AMEX, and NASDAQ markets—over 5,000 in all. It is designed to measure activity in all markets to best represent the overall health of the American economy.

The Wilshire 5000, which is prepared by Wilshire Associates, is not measured against the market itself but instead to a baseline value that was established at the end of 1980. In this way, the measurement of the markets' volatility can remain constant, even when circumstances may prevent the markets themselves from remaining so.

OTHER MEDIA

It would be virtually impossible to list all the sources of financial information. Financial information is presented on television on networks such as CNN, shows like *Moneyline,* and even the evening news, which has a segment to recap the daily trading activity. In addition, specialized financial magazines such as *Fortune, Inc.,* and *Forbes* provide even further information. Finally, the advent of technology has enabled the Internet to provide more, better, and faster financial information than could ever be used by one person.

PLAIN ENGLISH

Other media is a catchall phrase used to describe the various methods by which an investor can accumulate financial information. These include, but are not limited to, television and radio; publications such as newspapers, magazines, and newsletters; and the Internet.

The point is that, as an investor, one problem you should never encounter is a lack of resources with which to monitor the success of your investments. It is of the utmost importance to ensure that your efforts to digest some of this information do not turn investing into a grudging chore but rather an activity that is enjoyable and exciting. This enjoyment can be facilitated by using the media with which you are most comfortable. I, for example, don't like the time commitment involved in reading the newspaper—or the smudgy fingers. So, I leave the 24-hour news channel playing in the background while I'm getting dressed in the morning. I get my financial news with no fuss or bother this way.

You are certainly free to ignore the whole thing should you be so inclined, but, as stated earlier, the only one you cheat is yourself. Remember that this information is no longer esoteric or irrelevant to you. It is information with which you can evaluate and grow your investments and, subsequently, your money. It is information specifically geared to you, the investor.

THE 30-SECOND RECAP

- The ticker tape is still used in many electronic forms and contains such information as the stock's name, price, and the number of shares traded.

- Indices are an overall measurement of various markets. They are created by averaging the prices of representative stocks and applying internal adjustments as necessary.

- The Dow Jones Average is the most popular indicator of the U.S. stock market's health. One of its four components, the Dow Jones Industrial Average, is used synonymously with the New York Stock Exchange.

- Composite indices such as the NASDAQ National Market System Composite Index, the AMEX Market Value Index, and the New York Stock Exchange Composite Index measure their respective markets through the average of varying numbers of stock which are best thought to represent the respective market.

- Indices can range from the 30 that compose the Dow Jones Industrial Average to the 1,000 to 2,000 of the Russell indices to the biggest of them all, the Wilshire 5000 composed of all the quoted stocks on the NYSE, AMEX, and NASDAQ markets.

- Various media, including TV and radio, publications, and the Internet, provide a wealth of financial information and should be used freely by newer investors.

APPENDIX A

Glossary

52-week high-low   Entries in the daily stock tables of the highest and lowest point at which the stock has traded during the past year.

aggressive growth stocks   Stocks that focus on their potential for capital gains and accept higher principal risk to achieve this growth.

American Stock Exchange   Originally founded as the New York Curb Exchange in 1842, the American Stock Exchange is rivaled in prestige only by the New York Stock Exchange.

AMEX Market Value Index   An index composed of 800 stocks that trade on the American Stock Exchange. This type of index is based on the belief that the health of the American economy is best represented by the performance of the proprietary market.

asset   Anything owned that has value such as cash, real estate, intellectual property, or name recognition.

bankruptcy   A court declaration of the financial insolvency of a person or company.

blue chip stock   A designation for share of a company that is extremely well established and financially secure.

book value   A measurement of the total value of a company determined by adding up the values of all tangible assets. Or, the value of each share of common stock should the company declare bankruptcy, determined by dividing the value of the assets of a company by the number of its outstanding shares.

broker   Anyone who has received qualification to trade stock for clients by passing the Securities Exchange Commission's Series 7 Exam.

brokerage accounts   Monetary deposits maintained with a broker to trade stock.

buy and hold   An investment strategy characterized by purchasing stock to retain for an extended period of time. Additionally, buy and hold usually implies that dividends will be reinvested in subsequent purchases of the stock.

call   A contract that grants the bearer the option of purchasing stock for a predetermined price in the future regardless of the stock's actual market value at that time.

capital appreciation   The growth in the value of any type of investment asset such as stock or real estate.

capital gains   The total amount of profits from the sale of, or potential sale of, an investment asset.

cash account   A brokerage account stipulating that the investor can make no stock purchase larger than the amount of money within the account.

closing price   The amount at which the stock settled at the end of the trading day.

commodity futures   Contracts to buy or sell a specified amount of a product such as sugar, cotton, or precious metals for a predetermined price and date in the future. These contracts have value and are traded like stock.

common stock   A share of common stock is characterized by its owners receiving fluctuating dividends and voting one proxy per share.

compound interest   Interest paid as a percentage of the initial amount loaned and previous gains made with prior interest payments.

conservative growth stocks   Stocks that focus on their capital gains potential, but not at the expense of excessive capital risk.

constant dollar plan   An investment strategy in which the investor adds or subtracts cash to keep the number of original stock purchased constant.

corporate bond   An interest-paying certificate of indebtedness issued by a corporation to investors for the purposes of raising capital or cash.

credit limit   A predetermined maximum amount a person or company is entitled to borrow from a particular lender.

credit rating   A comprehensive data file of an individual's or a firm's past performance in the repayment of loans, or the ranking bestowed on that individual or firm by the credit rating company based on the same information. Also, evaluations by disinterested parties and services regarding the financial health of a company or individual.

current ratio   A projection of the company's ability to meet its financial obligations and remain solvent.

current yield   A formula that depicts the dividend payment of a stock as a percentage of the stock's market price.

custodial account   A brokerage account for a minor set up under the rules of the Uniform (Gifts) Transfers to Minors Act whereby an adult oversees the account's management on behalf of the minor until he or she becomes a legal adult.

daily high-low   Entries in the daily financial tables that list the highest and lowest point at which the stock traded over the course of the day.

debt   Anything owed.

debt ratio   A formula that compares a company's total debt to its assets and cash flows.

derivative   An investment that is based on a stock's performance.

discount broker   A broker who provides financial services individually rather than full service.

dividends   The portion of profits a company pays to its stockholders, usually in quarterly annual payments.

dividends per share   The amount of the last dividend paid.

dollar cost averaging   An investment strategy characterized by systematically investing a predetermined amount on a regular basis.

Dow Jones   A series of four separate indices that currently trades on the New York Stock Exchange and is considered by many to best represent the activity of the market and the American economy.

e-broker   A broker who provides financial self-service options online.

earnings per share   A company's net earnings divided by the number of its outstanding common shares.

evaluation   A projection of the future performance of the stock through the use of statistics and formulas.

financial media   Various methods by which an investor can accumulate financial information such as television, radio, newspapers, magazines, and the Internet.

full service broker   A broker who provides complete management over clients' accounts.

growth stock   Shares of a small company that is believed by its shareholders to have excellent potential to become larger.

income stocks   Shares of a company that focus on providing higher and more regular dividend payments over capital gains.

indices   A number of stocks whose prices are combined and averaged to demonstrate value changes in a particular market.

inflation   An economic condition in which prices rise resulting in a decrease in purchasing power.

inflation risk   The danger that your investment will not maintain its initial purchasing power because it is not growing as fast as the national inflation rate.

interest   An attached charge for the loan of money. The borrower pays, and the loaner receives, an amount above and beyond the initial amount loaned.

international markets   Stock exchanges in other countries.

liability   Anything owed, including bills, taxes, loans, or other financial obligations.

limit orders   Instructions to a broker to purchase stock at a price lower than the current market price or sell it at a price higher.

long-term capital gains   The total amount of profits from the sale of, or potential sale of, an investment asset that has been held more than one year.

margin account   A brokerage account that permits the purchase of stock with credit.

market order   Instructions to trade stock immediately at the best possible price. A market order is also known as an open order.

market price   The amount that can be received upon the sale of property.

market risk   The danger that a stock's performance will be influenced by conditions within the markets in which they trade.

miscellaneous information   Data in the daily stock tables such as currency exchange rates, IPO offerings, and analyst predictions.

money market   A mutual fund that invests in bank certificates of deposit, treasury bills, and loans to corporations that are considered particularly secure.

mutual fund   A variety of securities that are purchased with money pooled by a group of investors.

NASDAQ (National Association of Securities Dealers Automated Quotations system)   A computerized network over which brokers trade over-the-counter securities.

NASDAQ National Market System Composite Index   An index composed of over-the-counter stock traded on the NASDAQ system.

net change   The difference between a stock's current and previous day's closing price.

net worth   The total value of a company or an individual calculated by subtracting all liabilities from all assets.

New York Stock Exchange   Established in 1817, the NYSE is the largest and most prestigious stock exchange in the world.

New York Stock Exchange Index   An index composed of all 1,600 stocks trading at the New York Stock Exchange.

odd lots   Shares of stock that are purchased outside of a predetermined standard.

orders   Instructions to a broker on how stock should be traded.

options   A contract between two parties to trade stock at a predetermined price.

over-the-counter   Stocks that are traded over the largest stock trading network in this country, a computerized network known as NMS.

P/E ratio   A comparison of the current market value of the stock to its dividend payments.

penny stock   Highly speculative shares in a company with little or no real value other than uncertain growth potential.

political/governmental risk   The danger that domestic and international governmental actions will have ramifications affecting a stock's performance.

portfolio reevaluation   Periodic investment recalculations using newer and increased information to ensure the original decision is still correct or applicable.

preferred stock   A share of stock that is issued after common stock and whose dividends are a predetermined amount and paid prior to common stock's dividends.

puts   A contract that grants the option of selling stock at a predetermined price in the future regardless of the stock's actual market value at that time.

principal   The initial amount of money used to purchase an investment.

qualifiers   Symbols and initials on the stock tables that denote circumstances associated with the corresponding stock information.

recommendation   A request for, or the receipt of, information or insight from a person who may have a better insight into the stock's future performance.

regional exchange   One of 14 exchanges around the United States that offer the larger stocks of the NYSE or AMEX and proprietary-listed stock for trade.

research   Checking sources for information on a stock and/or its performance.

round lots   A predetermined number of shares of stock that is considered standard for trade.

Russell Indices   Three indices that rate the activities of stocks, based on their market capitalization. The smallest, the Russell 1000, measures the activities of the 1,000 largest capitalized companies, while the Russell 2000 measures those of the less capitalized companies.

secondary stock   Shares of a company with substantial backing that is not considered blue chip.

short-term capital gains   The total amount of profits from the sale of, or potential sale of, an investment asset that has been held for one year or less.

speculate   To take greater risks when investing in order to make larger gains.

speculative stocks   Stocks that have little or no real value other than unsupported potential (for example, long shots).

Standard and Poor's 500   An index composed of the 500 largest stocks trading on the NYSE and the NASDAQ.

stock   A representation of partial ownership of a company. A stock can be either a physical document or a computerized account.

stock market   Centralized physical locations or computer networks over which stock is traded.

stock name   An entry in the daily stock table, usually in the form of abbreviations and acronyms.

stock symbol   An entry in the daily stock tables of the symbols used to identify a stock, composed of one- to four-letter combinations.

stop orders   Instructions to a broker to sell stock at a price lower than the current market value or buy it at a price higher than the current market value.

subscription right   An option granted to current shareholders to buy future-issued stock at a discount price.

tax-free bond   A bond issued by state or local government to investors for raising capital or cash of which interest is exempt from municipal, state, and/or federal taxes.

ticker tape   Originally an actual machine; the term is currently used to describe an electronic ribbon which carries information on currently occurring stock trades.

time notations   Instructions to a broker regarding how long an order should remain in effect.

    GTW   Good Through the Week.

    GTM   Good Through the Month.

    GTC   Good unTil Canceled.

Treasury securities   U.S. government obligations that are available for purchase to the public through Federal Reserve banks. Investments of this type include Treasury bills (T-bills), bonds, certificates, and notes.

utility stock   Shares in a company that provides public service such as gas or electricity.

Vol 100s   An entry in the daily stock tables of the number of total shares traded that day. The figure in this column must be multiplied by 100 when under 10,000 for the correct number of traded shares.

warrant   A contract issued by a company to purchase its stock at a predetermined price regardless of the market value of the stock at that time.

Wilshire 5000 Index   An index composed of all quoted stocks on the NYSE, AMEX, and NASDAQ markets, over 5,000 in all. It is designed to measure activity in all markets to best represent the overall health of the American economy and is the largest of all popular indices.

Yield Percent   The ratio of dividends paid by a stock to its closing price which is used to depict the amount of income generated by the stock relevant to its initial investment requirement.

APPENDIX B
Resources

CREDIT REPORTING AGENCIES

While other credit reporting agencies do exist, the following two are the most commonly utilized by everyone. A personal copy of your credit file is made available upon request.

Experion

P.O. Box 949

Allen, TX 75013-0949

1-888-397-3742

Trans Union

P.O. Box 403

Springfield, PA 19064-0403

1-800-916-8800

FINANCIAL MEDIA

Almost all local newspapers of any reasonable size run stock tables daily. In addition, several general newspapers such as *The New York Times* and financial newspapers such as *The Wall Street Journal* run national editions available through subscription virtually anywhere. A quick trip to your local bookstore or library will provide discovery of so many magazines that focus exclusively on various aspects of finance that a comprehensive list would be impossible. Several of the more popular financial magazines are listed here with contact information, should you find them unavailable on your local newsstand.

Also, please be aware that all daily television news programs run a section on the day's trading. More comprehensive pictures of stock market activity are available through television shows such as *Moneyline* as well as dedicated financial networks such as CFNN.

The New York Times
229 W. 43rd Street
New York, NY 10036
1-800-639-8463

The Financial Times
1330 Avenue of the Americas
New York, NY 10019
1-800-628-8088; www.ft.com

The Wall Street Journal
200 Liberty Street
New York, NY 10281
1-800-568-7625; www.wsj.com

Investment News
220 E. 42nd Street
New York, NY 10017-5846
212-210-0114; www.investmentnews.com

Forbes Magazine
60 5th Avenue
New York, NY 10011
1-800-888-9896; www.forbes.com

Fortune
P.O. Box 60001
Tampa, FL 33660
1-800-621-8000; www.fortune.com

Salomon Smith Barney
1-888-SERIOUS; www.smithbarney.com

Prudential Investment Management
751 Broad Street
Newark, NJ 07102-3777
1-800-THE ROCK; www.prudential.com

BROKERS

The following list is neither comprehensive nor should be considered a recommendation for any of the listed brokers. It is supplied only to give you a starting point from which to search for your own broker or brokerage account. Almost all these brokers offer services ranging from full service to online trading. You will need to determine the services that are most applicable to your own needs. In addition to this national contact information, you should check your local Yellow Pages under Investment Management.

Goldman Sachs
1-877-813-2445; www.goldmansachs.com

Donaldson, Lufkin & Jenrette (DLJ Direct)
1-800-355 -8888; www.dljdirect.com

National Discount Brokers
1-800-417-7423; www.ndb.com

TD Waterhouse
www.tdwaterhouse.com

Barclays Global Investors
415-597-2000; www.barclaysglobal.com

Ameritrade
1-800-454-9272; www.ameritrade.com

J.P. Morgan
212-648-9607; www.jpmorgan.com

Salomon Smith Barney
212-816-6000; www.smithbarney.com

Morgan Stanley Dean Witter
1-800-240-3932; www.morganstanley.com

Wall Street Access
1-800-925-5782; www.wallstreetaccess.com

Fidelity Investments
1-800-343-3548; www.fidelity.com

ONLINE RESEARCH

Nothing since the introduction of money has affected finance as significantly as the Internet. In addition to the Web sites listed with each broker, the following listed browsers and home pages have extensive finance areas ranging from topics as basic as budgeting to extensive topics such as macroeconomics. They also offer chat rooms, where you can speak to other investors, and portfolio management, where you can list and track your investments. In addition, these pages, as well as the independent research sites listed, all provide daily news that may affect your investments and offer free e-newsletter subscriptions. Again, this list is neither comprehensive nor a recommendation, but simply a push in the right direction.

www.netscape.com	www.yahoo.com
www.aol.com	www.finance.com
www.goto.com	www.thestreet.com
www.lycos.com	www.stockjungle.com
www.altavista.com	

INDEX

T

U–V

W–Z